Written by Samantha Barnes, Dominique Enright,
Guy Macdonald and Matthew Morgan
Illustrated by Niki Catlow
Cover illustration by John Bigwood

The material in this book was taken from three titles previously published by Buster Books:
Children's Miscellany Volume One, Children's Miscellany Volume Two
and *Children's Miscellany Volume Three.*

First published in Great Britain in 2015 by Buster Books,
an imprint of Michael O'Mara Books Limited
9 Lion Yard, Tremadoc Road, London SW4 7NQ

 www.busterbooks.co.uk Buster Children's Books @BusterBooks

A CIP catalogue record for this book is available from the British Library.

ISBN 978-1-78055-316-0

2 4 6 8 10 9 7 5 3 1

Printed and bound in August 2015 by CPI Group
(UK) Ltd, Croydon, CR0 4YY

Papers used by Buster Books are natural, recyclable products
made from wood grown in sustainable forests. The manufacturing processes
conform to environmental regulations of the country of origin.

NOTE TO READERS
The publisher and authors disclaim any liability for accidents or injuries
that may occur as a result of information given in this book.
Every effort has been made to ensure that the information in this book
is correct at the time of going to press. Nevertheless, some of the
information is, by its very nature, anecdotal, changeable or disputable,
and cannot therefore be assumed to be authoritative or exhaustive.
The book is, however, guaranteed to be thoroughly enjoyable.

Buster Books

If you're reading this page you must be a clever kid who wants to know more ...

This book is full of fascinating facts, some serious and some bizarre. There are snippets of gruesome history, jaw-dropping geography and stunning science. You'll find brain teasers, optical illusions and cool tricks to master. Just open the book at any page and enjoy the brilliant, brain-boosting and bite-sized bits of information.

There's an index at the back of the book to guide you to anything you particularly want to find out about.

LIFETIME AVERAGES

Time spent on the toilet..6 months

Time spent eating..3 years

Time spent waiting for things.......................................3 years

Time spent talking..10 years

Time spent sleeping...22 years

Number of times fingers bent and straightened..........25 million

Number of smells remembered...................................10,000

Distance travelled on foot.......................22,500 km (14,000 miles)

Length of hair grown.................................1,000 km (621 miles)

Volume of tears shed.....................................65 l (14.3 gal)

Number of balloons you could fill with exhaled air..............14 million

Litres of blood pumped round body..............380,000 l (100,000 gal)

Number of cells produced........................750,000 billion

TRICKS FOR WINNING AT CONKERS

Don't use conkers that float in water.

Keep your conker wrapped in cloth for a year or more.

Soak your conker in vinegar.

Bake your conker in the oven.

Coat your conker with nail varnish.

CRYPTIDS

(Animals that have been rumoured but not proven to exist.)

ORANG PENDEK
A mysteriously human-like
ape from Sumatra covered
in thick dark hair, with
a long mane and a
hairless brown face.

CHUPACABRA
A bloodsucking beast
from Central America that
walks on two legs, has
large black eyes and
attacks goats and cattle.

MONGOLIAN DEATH WORM
A 4-foot-long red worm
from the Gobi desert that
can kill instantly from
several feet away, by
shooting poison or electric
currents at its prey.

THUNDERBIRD
A huge bird with
a wingspan of over 6 m
(20 ft) that is said to have
appeared in a photograph
in the Wild West but has
since disappeared.

TRUNKO
A whale-sized furry
sea mammal with an
elephantine trunk, said to
have washed up on the
coast of South Africa.

SUCURIJU GIGANTE
A giant anaconda around
12 m (40 ft) long
that lives in the
Amazon rainforest.

DOUBLE-JOINTEDNESS

One in every 20 people is double-jointed in some way. The medical term for it is 'joint hypermobility', meaning that a person's joint has been formed in such a way as to allow for extra movement – it's actually nothing to do with having 'double' of anything. If you have these very flexible joints you might be able to:

Touch your wrist with the thumb of the same hand.

Bend your elbows backwards.

Lie on your stomach with your feet touching your head.

Bend over and put your shoulders between your knees.

Join your hands behind your back and lift them over
your head without letting go.

DISGUSTING AND DANGEROUS PLANTS

STINKY FLOWERS
The rafflesia and titan arum plants smell horribly of rotting meat.

PITCHER PLANTS
This plant has leaves in the shape of tubular jugs. Insects fall in and cannot climb out.

FLYPAPER
The sundew has sticky hairs on its leaves, which trap insects that the plant then digests.

VENUS FLYTRAP
Has a hinged leaf with two spiked lobes like scary jaws. The lobes snap shut on any small beast that might venture into the 'mouth', and do not reopen until the creature has been digested.

STRANGLER
This type of fig tree produces roots above ground, which wrap themselves around other trees ... or whatever else gets in their way.

COOL TRANSPORT

Skateboards • Roller skates • Ice skates • Space hoppers
Pogo sticks • Scooters • Bicycles • Tricycles • Unicycles

THINGS TO DRESS UP AS
WHEN RUNNING A MARATHON

Gorilla • Sumo wrestler • Rhinoceros • A cottage • Chicken

Viking longboat • Cornish pasty • Pantomime horse

Deep-sea diver (including lead boots)

HOW TO GET RID – 'HIC' – OF HICCUPS

Bend over at the waist and drink water from the further side of a glass (that is, with your chin stuck in the glass).

Hold your breath for at least a minute.

Try to swallow a spoonful of peanut butter.

Pull hard on your tongue.

Place a spoonful of sugar at the back of your tongue; repeat two to three times as necessary.

Suck on a piece of fresh lemon.

Take a deep breath and hold it while squeezing your stomach muscles as hard as possible.

THE AFTERLIFE

RELIGION	FOR THE GOOD	FOR THE WICKED
Ancient Greek	Elysium	Hades
Ancient Egyptian	Yaru	Eaten by Devourer
Christianity	Heaven	Hell
Islam	Paradise	Jahannam
Judaism	Garden of Eden	She'ol / Gehenna
Buddhism	Nirvana	Reincarnation as a worm

FUNNY BONES

Number of bones babies have...300

Number of bones adults have...206

Number of bones in hands and feet...106

Number of bones in head..22

Smallest bone...Stirrup bone, ear (2.5 mm, 0.1 in)

Longest bone.....................Femur, thigh (a quarter of a person's height)

Hardest bone..............................Petrous temporal bone, base of skull

Only bone not connected to another..................Hyoid, base of tongue

YUOR AZAMNIG MNID

Sceitnsits hvae dsicveored taht the hmuan biran is so uesd to raednig taht it deosn't mtater waht oredr the letetrs are in, as lnog as you mkae srue the frist and lsat ltteers are in the rhgit pclae. Tihs is bcuease we raed the wlhoe wrod, rthaer tahn ecah ltteer. In fcat, eevn thguoh the mdilde leettrs are jmulbed up, yuor biarn is pobrbaly cveelr eognuh to raed tihs wouthit too mcuh truolbe.

WISE WORDS

Don't pick on your sister when she's holding a hockey stick.

If you want a kitten, start out by asking for a horse.

If you get a bad school report, wait until your mum's
on the phone to show it to her.

When your dad is mad at you and asks 'Do I look stupid?'
- don't answer him.

When you want something expensive, ask your grandparents.

Never tell your little sister that you're not going
to do what your mum told you to do.

Always look busy with homework when your mum shows
up with a dustpan and brush or vacuum cleaner.

Never dare your little brother to paint the family car.

ARCHENEMIES OF SUPERHEROES

Lex Luthor..Superman

The Joker...Batman

Green Goblin..Spider-Man

Shredder........................Teenage Mutant Ninja Turtles

Cheetah...Wonder Woman

Sabretooth..Wolverine

Loki..Thor

MORSE CODE ALPHABET

A	.-	H	....	O	---	V	...-
B	-...	I	..	P	.--.	W	.--
C	-.-.	J	.---	Q	--.-	X	-..-
D	-..	K	-.-	R	.-.	Y	-.--
E	.	L	.-..	S	...	Z	--..
F	..-.	M	--	T	-		
G	--.	N	-.	U	..-		

DOWN THE HATCH

Keep a piece of bread in your mouth for a few minutes and after a short while you'll notice a sweet taste. That is the beginning of digestion, as enzymes in your saliva begin to dissolve the food and break down the carbohydrates into sugar.

The next step is when you swallow the food - down it goes into the stomach - a churning pool of hydrochloric acid, which is so concentrated that if you were to put a drop onto a piece of wood, it would eat right through it (luckily your stomach protects itself with a bicarbonate lining). The acid and more enzymes work on the food to break it down further.

Then the food is pushed into the 5 m long (about 18 ft - longer in an adult) coiled-up small intestine, and is squeezed along the length of it. More digestive juices - from the pancreas and liver - pour on to the food particles before, at last, they are pushed out of the small intestine.

By now the body has extracted from the bits of food all that it needs in the way of nutrients, and the food is in the large intestine (three times wider than the small, but only about 1.5 m, or 5 ft, long). There, any remaining water is sucked out of the food and it descends as a lump of brown waste to join more brown waste at the bottom of the large intestine. And there it waits until ...

... the owner of the intestines hurries off to the loo.

THINGS THAT HAVE RAINED FROM THE SKY

Frogs

Squid

Hermit crabs

Jellyfish

Worms

Corn

Sardines

Coloured rain

Catfish

Baby alligators

Butterflies

Beer cans

WHAT GREEN MEANS

Growth • Spring • New life • Youth • Inexperience • Hope
Prosperity • Relaxation • Passivity • Receptivity • Harmony
Reassurance • Safety • Envy • Jealousy

WHO IS THAT RELATIVE?

Half-brother/sister...Shares one parent with you

Stepmum/dad...Your parent's wife/husband

Stepbrother/sister...Your stepmum/dad's child

First cousin...Your aunt or uncle's child

Second cousin...Your parent's cousin's child

Third cousin.................................Your grandparent's cousin's grandchild

First cousin once removed...Your parent's cousin

OR your cousin's child

First cousin twice removed.................................Your grandparent's cousin

OR your cousin's grandchild

Second cousin once removed...................Your parent's second cousin

OR your second cousin's child

—— DISEASES YOU REALLY DON'T WANT TO CATCH ——

YELLOW FEVER
5-40% of sufferers die –
caught from mosquitoes.
Starts with a fever,
vomiting and sore eyes.
Death from organ failure.

LASSA FEVER
20% die if left untreated –
caught from rats. Death
from brain inflammation
and bleeding.

BUBONIC PLAGUE
15-60% die – starts
with a sore throat,
fever and headache.
Leads to abscesses,
gangrene and fits.

NECROTIZING FASCIITIS
15-50% die – caught from
other people. Death by
flesh-eating killer bug
unless all infected areas
are cut out.

EBOLA VIRUS
50% die – starts with
a rash, fever and headache.
Death from bleeding
and coma.

CHOLERA
50% die if left untreated –
caught from poo-infected
water. Begins with diarrhoea
and vomiting. Death from
dehydration and organ failure.

MARBURG DISEASE
50-90% die – caught from
monkeys. Death from kidney,
liver, lung or brain failure.

RABIES
100% die if left untreated.
Result of being bitten
by an infected animal.
Leads to madness and
inflammation of the brain.

—— THE BEST WAY TO MAKE YOURSELF DIZZY ——

Bend over and hold your left ankle with your right hand,
then spin anti-clockwise.

THE ORIGINS OF THE SALUTE

In Roman times, when assassination and murder were rife, or even well before, it was the custom to greet someone by holding up an empty hand – to show that you were not carrying a weapon.

Medieval knights would similarly show an empty hand as an indication that they meant no harm. They would also lift up the visors of their helmets to show their face.

The removal of a helmet or other headgear indoors was a sign of respect which, applied to hats of all kinds, has been carried on through the centuries.

SEVEN WONDERS OF THE ANCIENT WORLD

Great Pyramids of Egypt

Hanging Gardens of Babylon

Temple of Artemis at Ephesus

Statue of Zeus at Olympia

Mausoleum at Halicarnassus

Colossus of Rhodes

Lighthouse of Alexandria

SEVEN WONDERS OF THE NATURAL WORLD

Aurora Borealis (Northern Lights)

Mount Everest

Harbour of Rio de Janeiro

The Great Barrier Reef

Victoria Falls

The Grand Canyon

Paricutin Volcano

THE FIVE STAGES OF SLEEP

LIGHT SLEEP - During this period you are half-awake and half-asleep. For about ten minutes you can easily be awakened. People can take 'cat naps' with their eyes open without even being aware of it.

TRUE SLEEP - This lasts for about 20 minutes. While you are asleep your body produces large amounts of growth hormones that help repair or replace damaged cells, and chemicals important to the immune system - thus speeding up healing and keeping you healthy.

DEEP SLEEP - Your brainwave patterns slow down. The slower the brainwaves, the deeper the sleep. Sleep gives your brain a chance to organize the previous day's events and file away memories. Lack of sleep makes you irritable, forgetful, inattentive, unable to make judgements, uncoordinated and more likely to fall ill. Severe sleep deprivation causes paranoia, delusions and hallucinations.

DEEPER SLEEP - Your breathing becomes slow and rhythmic, and your muscles are barely active.

REM (RAPID EYE MOVEMENT) - 70 to 90 minutes after you fall asleep you start dreaming. Your eyes move about, your brain becomes very active, and your breathing rate and blood pressure rise; your muscles relax so much that your body seems unable to move. Most dreams last six to ten minutes, but can last longer. The record is 150 minutes. Happy dreams are more common; any nightmares you might have usually come towards morning.

Rubber bands last longer if you keep them in the fridge.

The longest recorded flight of a chicken is 13 seconds.

MYSTERIES AT SEA

THE FLYING DUTCHMAN

The Flying Dutchman is a phantom ship condemned to sail the oceans with a ghostly crew. The ship has been sighted many times. The last recorded sighting was in 1942, off the coast of Cape Town, South Africa.

THE BERMUDA TRIANGLE

The Bermuda Triangle is a mysterious area in the Atlantic Ocean where paranormal events and unexplained disappearances are alleged to occur. Some say the Bermuda Triangle is inhabited by monsters that kidnap ships and aircraft.

ATLANTIS

According to ancient myth, Atlantis is the name of a lost island that sank into the ocean after tidal waves covered it in water. Explorers have travelled over the globe in search of traces of its existence, but no real evidence has ever been discovered.

THE MARY CELESTE

The Mary Celeste was found adrift on the Atlantic Ocean in 1872. The ship was in first-class condition and there was plenty of food and water. The crew, however, had disappeared.

WHAT KIND OF MANIAC ARE YOU?

(Maniac: a person who is obsessed with something)

Pyromaniac..Fire

Balletomaniac...Ballet

Islomaniac..Islands

Egomaniac...Yourself

Bibliomaniac..Books

Anthomaniac..Flowers

Graphomaniac..Writing

Dromomaniac...Running

Monomaniac..One thing

Mythomaniac...Lying

EARLY BRAIN SURGERY

Trepanning was a medical practice used as long ago as 7,000 BC to treat bad headaches, head injuries, seizures and possession by evil spirits.

A hole was cut into the skull using a stone axe or a knife. As there was no anaesthetic, the patient was either knocked out or held down to prevent them running away. How well the surgery worked is debatable, but in a great many cases the patient survived and was presumably restored to health, as the holes in skulls found by archaeologists can be seen to have partially repaired themselves.

Trepanning continued to be practised from the Stone Age, through ancient civilizations such as those of Egypt, Greece, Rome and the new Islamic civilization, through medieval times and beyond. And it still is today, generally in cases where there is bleeding between the brain and the skull, as this can produce too much pressure on the brain and even cause death. Afterwards the hole is fitted with a neat metal disc in place of the removed bone.

THE SILENT ALPHABET

A as in bread

B as in debt

C as in indictment
(pronounced 'in-dite-ment')

D as in handkerchief

E as in give

F as in halfpenny
(pronounced 'hay-penny')

G as in gnaw

H as in hour

I as in friend

J as in rijsttafel (a cold buffet
pronounced 'rice-taffel')

K as in know

L as in calm

M as in the first m
in mnemonic

N as in autumn

O as in people

P as in psalm

Q as in Colquhoun
(a Scottish surname
pronounced 'Co'hoon')

R as in forecastle
(pronounced 'fo'csle')

S as in island

T as in castle

U as in guard

V as in Milngavie
(a Scottish place name
pronounced 'Mull-ga'i')

W as in wrong

X as in Sioux
(pronounced 'Soo')

Y as in Pepys
(pronounced 'Peeps')

Z as in rendezvous

THE MOZART EFFECT

The Mozart Effect is a phrase used to mean that music has a beneficial effect on health, happiness and education. This seems a reasonable assessment – except that some people got over-excited by scientists' reports, and interpreted them to mean that listening to Mozart magically makes you more clever. For the last ten years or more the Mozart Effect has been argued about. There is no reason to believe that listening to Mozart will raise your overall IQ – but you might well find that listening to many kinds of music makes you feel happier, calmer and less stressed, so you can think more clearly and work better.

WHEN SHOULD YOU SNEEZE?

Sneeze on Monday,
sneeze for danger;

Sneeze on Tuesday,
kiss a stranger;

Sneeze on Wednesday,
get a letter;

Sneeze on Thursday,
something better;

Sneeze on Friday,
sneeze for sorrow;

Sneeze on Saturday,
see your sweetheart tomorrow;

Sneeze on Sunday, your safety seek, for the Devil will
have you the whole of the week.

The longest sneezing bout ever recorded was that of a 12-year-old British girl named Donna Griffiths, who started sneezing on 13 January 1981 and averaged a sneeze a minute for the first year, then slowed down to a sneeze about every five minutes. This went on until 16 September 1983: 978 days.

It's impossible to lick your elbow.

COMPUTER BYTES

1 byte = 8 binary digits (bits)

1 kilobyte (Kb) = 1,024 bytes

1 megabyte (Mb) = 1,024 Kb

1 gigabyte (Gb) = 1,024 Mb

1 terabyte (Tb) = 1,024 Gb

WHAT IS AIR?

78.00% nitrogen

21.00% oxygen

0.03% carbon dioxide

0.07% other

POINTLESS INSTRUCTIONS

On a blanket from Taiwan:
'Not to be used as protection
from a tornado.'

*On a helmet-mounted
mirror used by US cyclists:*
'Remember, objects
in the mirror are
actually behind you.'

*On the bottle top of
a flavoured milk drink:*
'After opening, keep upright.'

On a packet of crisps:
'You could be a winner.
No purchase necessary.
Details inside.'

On a packet of peanuts:
'Warning – contains nuts.'

On a Korean kitchen knife:
'Warning: keep out
of children.'

*On a string of Chinese-made
Christmas lights:*
'For indoor or outdoor
use only.'

*On a Japanese
food processor:*
'Not to be used for
the other use.'

*On a tiramisu dessert
(on the bottom of the box):*
'Do not turn upside down.'

On a Superman costume:
'Wearing this garment does
not enable you to fly.'

WHAT TO DO IF ZOMBIES ATTACK

- Act fast - zombies multiply very quickly.

- Dress in protective bite-proof clothing (e.g. leather).

- Follow the news to find out which areas are safe and which are most dangerous.

- Rescue as many survivors as possible - there's safety in numbers.

- Make sure none of the survivors have been secretly bitten - they may become zombies and turn on you later.

- Zombies are slow, so run for it.

- Zombies are also stupid, so confuse them by changing direction and creating diversions.

- Make sure you have plenty of food and water supplies (a supermarket makes an ideal shelter).

- Lock all doors and windows and pile heavy objects against them for extra security.

- Remember zombies can only be killed by destroying their brain, so don't waste energy fighting them.

> The following sentence is false. The preceding sentence is true. Are these sentences true or false?

Answer: It's neither true nor false - it's a paradox.

WHAT IS A GOOGOL?

A googol is 1 followed by 100 zeros.

Because this takes a long time to write and it is easy to lose count of all those zeros, we say: 10 to the power of 100. This is written 10^{100}.

A googolplex is 10 to the power of a googol - or 10 to the power of 10 to the power of 100. This is written $10^{10^{100}}$.
It is not a number for which there is much demand.

COCKNEY RHYMING SLANG

Apples (apples and pears)	Stairs
Dog (dog and bone)	Phone
Plates (plates of meat)	Feet
Scarper (Scapa Flow)	Go, i.e. run away
Titfer (tit for tat)	Hat
Trouble (trouble and strife)	Wife
Baker's (baker's dozen)	Cousin
Butcher's (butcher's hook)	Look
Half-inch	Pinch, i.e. steal
Pork chop	Cop, i.e. police officer
Skin (skin and blister)	Sister
Tea leaf	Thief
Whistle (whistle and flute)	Suit (garment)

MEN WHO WERE WOMEN

GEORGE ELIOT (1819-1876)
Actually called Mary Ann Evans, this novelist used a male pen-name so that her work would be taken seriously.

ANNE BONNEY AND MARY READ (early 1700s)
These pirates disguised themselves as men because at the time sailors believed it was bad luck to have a woman on board a ship.

LE BLANC (1776-1831)
Sophie Germain presented a mathematics paper that was so impressive the professor sought out this 'student'. The professor was amazed to find that 'he' was a young Frenchwoman and entirely self-taught.

JAMES BARRY (1795-1865)
A surgeon in the British Army, James was discovered to have been a woman only at 'his' death.

WOULD YOU RATHER ...

... have your legs sewn on backwards or live with
a second head on your body?

... be banished to outer space or the centre of the Earth?

... own a hamster as big as a dog, or a dog as
small as a hamster?

... squeak when you walk or blow bubbles when you talk?

... be three feet taller or three feet shorter?

... use a chainsaw as a toothbrush or a chainsaw for a nail file?

... talk like Yoda or breathe like Darth Vader for
the rest of your life?

... have a body covered with scales or a
body covered with fur?

... be covered in treacle and stung to death by bees
or be covered in honey and eaten by bears?

... be able to fly or be able to travel through time?

... have a theme tune for all of your actions for the
rest of your life or have no reflection?

VEGETABLES WHICH ARE IN FACT FRUITS

Tomatoes • Cucumbers • Aubergines • Courgettes • Peppers
Chillis • Avocados • Squashes • Pumpkins • Peapods

NELSON'S BODY PARTS

This is a game to play with a group of friends. You should wait in an empty room and ask your friends to take it in turns to come and knock at the door. When you hear the knock, meet your friend at the door and put a blindfold on them. Tell them that various things belonging to Admiral Nelson have been found at sea, and that it is their job to identify them. It might help them to know that Nelson lost an arm and an eye in land battles (but still went on to fight for his country at sea despite suffering from sea sickness!). Put the following things into your friend's hands and ask them what they think they are:

Your elbow = Nelson's partial arm
(bend your arm and let your friend touch the
top of your elbow)

A boot = Nelson's shoe

A hat = Nelson's admiral's hat

A peeled grape = Nelson's eye

The person who guesses the least correctly should be summoned back to the room, and made to eat Nelson's eye.

A spider's web is made of two types of thread, one sticky and the other not. The spider makes the non-sticky spokes first, then builds the sticky spiral part onto the frame. The spider walks on the spokes and avoids the sticky strands.

THINGS TO PUT IN A TIME CAPSULE

A lock of your hair.

Today's newspaper.

A picture of you and your best friend.

A description of what you think the future will be like.

An item connected with your favourite hobby.

An MP3 player with your favourite song on it.

VERY STRANGE GAMES

Cheese rolling, England and Italy

Cup stacking, USA

Wife carrying, Finland and Estonia

Zorbing (rolling around in an inflatable sphere), New Zealand

Cowpat tossing, Oklahoma, USA

Bog snorkelling, international

Cockroach racing, Australia

Biplane wing walking, international

DOGS' WORK

HERDING	HUNTING	GUARDING	RETRIEVING
Afghan hound	Beagle	Doberman	Labrador
Alsatian	Borzoi	Lhasa apso	Poodle
Border collie	Chow	Schipperke	Curly-coated
Puli	Greyhound	Bernese	retriever
Samoyed	Jack Russell	mountain dog	Golden retriever

THINGS YOU WISH YOU DIDN'T KNOW ABOUT THE ROMANS

They had ten-seater communal toilets. As there was no toilet paper, they shared a wet sponge on a stick.

They didn't use soap. They covered their bodies with oil and scraped off the dirt.

They washed their clothes (and sometimes their hair) in urine to get the grease out.

They cleaned their teeth with a mixture of powdered mouse brains, honey, and ashes made by burning dogs' teeth.

Although it was illegal, some Romans sold their children as slaves if they didn't like them.

Roman doctors were trained to ignore the screams of soldiers, and would amputate their arms or legs without any painkillers.

WHO IS DOCTOR WHO?

Name:	Unknown
Aliases:	Dr Who (from the question in the first episode: 'Who is he? Doctor who?'), Ka Faraq Gatri, Bringer of Darkness Destroyer of Worlds
Profession:	Time Lord
Planet of Origin:	Gallifrey
Date of Birth:	Unknown. First appearance, 100,000 BC
Life Expectancy:	Many many centuries
Physical Powers:	Can regenerate injured or old parts of body
Transport:	TARDIS: Time And Relative Dimension In Space (time machine in the shape of 1950s-era police box)
Enemies:	The Master (another Time Lord) The Daleks (mutants created during a war between the Kaleds and the Thals, soft and repulsive in appearance, who have to live inside mechanical tank-like casings and are bent on universal destruction) Davros (the evil wheelchair-bound scientist who created the Daleks)
Famous Friends:	Leonardo da Vinci, William Shakespeare, H. G. Wells, Winston Churchill, Charles Dickens

CAPITAL CITIES YOU MIGHT NOT KNOW

Apia, Samoa • Nuuk, Greenland

Nuku'alofa, Tonga • Majuro, Marshall Islands

Thimphu, Bhutan • Roseau, Dominica • Paramaribo, Suriname

Nouakchott, Mauritania • Ouagadougou, Burkina Faso

Podgorica, Montenegro

MAN OR MONKEY?

Apes and humans share 98 per cent of their genetic material.
However, there are some differences:

APE	MAN
• Small brain	• Large, variable-sized brain
• Arms longer than legs	• Legs longer than arms
• Hand-like feet with opposable big toes	• Feet for walking, not climbing
• Walks on all fours	• Walks upright
• Spine joins skull from back	• Spine joins skull from below
• Knee joints will not lock upright	• Knee joints lock upright
• Very hairy body	• Short hair over most of the body
• Completely brown eyes	• Mostly white eyes
• Vocal cords only capable of simple sounds.	• Vocal cords capable of complex sounds and singing.

——————— LESSONS TO LEARN FROM CARTOONS ———————

- When running off a cliff, you will run some way in mid-air before stopping, looking down and plummeting to the ground.

- When wishing to arrive unnoticed by burrowing underground, you will leave a trail of dirt above ground for all to see.

- If hit in the face with an object (e.g. an iron), your face will flatten and take on the shape of that object.

- If you swallow an object (e.g. a birdcage), your body will take on the shape of that object.

- When you hit the ground after a fall from a great height, you will create a huge fog of dust and a crater in the ground that is the exact shape of your body.

- If you are surprised, your eyes will jump out of their sockets, your feet will come away from the floor and a trumpet will sound in the background.

- If you see someone beautiful, your pupils will turn into love hearts and your heart will pump so hard it can be seen moving in and out of your chest.

- Whatever you buy or build in order to catch your opponent (especially if bought from ACME) will not work. It is likely to malfunction and cause extensive damage to you.

- If run over by heavy machinery, particularly a steam roller, you will be completely flattened. You will, however, be able to prize your flattened shape from the ground and pop back into shape soon after.

SECRETS OF SNOT

Snot is mucus – a slimy substance produced by plants and animals.

Snot keeps things running smoothly, like engine oil in a car.

Snot traps any dust and objects (including small insects) that might go up your nostrils.

Bogeys are dried-up, dust- and germ-filled bits of snot.

Sneezing blasts out snot at 160 kph (100 mph).

When you have a cold your body produces extra snot to rid itself of invading viruses.

When your snot turns into nasty-coloured thick catarrh it is usually because an infection has taken hold and your body is fighting against it.

EGYPTIAN GODS AND THEIR ANIMAL FORMS

Amun............The Supreme God............Ram

Anubis............God of the Dead............Jackal

Bast............Daughter of the Sun God Ra............Cat

Horus............God of the Sky............Falcon

Mut............Queen of All Gods............Vulture

Sekhmet............Goddess of War............Lioness

Seth............God of Chaos and Evil............Monster

Thoth............God of the Moon and Wisdom............Ibis

Hathor............Goddess of Love and Nurture............Cow

THE SIMPSONS

'Doh' now appears in the online version of the
Oxford English Dictionary.

Matt Groening named the characters after his own family:
his father is called Homer, his mother is Margaret (Marge),
one sister is Lisa, another is Maggie. Bart is an anagram
of 'brat', which is a rhyming reference to himself, Matt.

Matt Groening named his sons,
born in 1991 and 1993, Homer and Abe.

Look at Homer from the side and you can see
that the zigzag of his hair forms an 'M' for Matt,
and his ear forms a 'G' for Groening.

In one episode Lisa gives her email address as
'smart girl six three underscore backslash at Yahoo dot com'
(smartgirl63_\@yahoo.com).

Among the store names of Springfield are a law company
called I Can't Believe It's A Law Firm!; a toy store called
J. R. R. Toykins; a pastry shop called The French Confection;
a seafood restaurant called The Fryin' Dutchman, and
the comic book store, Android's Dungeon.

Krusty the Clown's real name is Herschel Schmoikel Krustofski.

In one episode, two area codes are given
that would locate half of Springfield in Missouri and half
in Puerto Rico (an island)! Elsewhere, we are told that Springfield
is 1,091.14 km (678 miles) from Mexico City and 4,269.59 km
(2,653 miles) from Orlando, Florida - an impossibility.

Springfield's official motto is 'Corruptus in Extremis',
and the motto of the mystery state in which it lies
within is 'Not just another state'.

Strawberries have more Vitamin C than oranges.

BITS OF BRAIN

Your brain is divided into three main bits:

1. The brain stem to the back of your head, at the bottom, which deals with automatic actions like breathing and digestion.

2. The cerebellum at the back, which controls and coordinates day-to-day actions such as walking.

3. The cerebrum at the front, which plans and controls movements, interprets the messages it receives from your eyes, ears, tongue, fingertips, etc, and remembers, thinks and solves problems. The right-hand side is more involved in creative and artistic activities; the left-hand side is used for logical or mathematical processes.

LANGUAGE FAMILIES

Number of languages in the world...6,000+

Number of language families...12

Biggest language family...Indo-European

Second biggest language family.......................................Sino-Tibetan

Most difficult language to learn..Basque

WHAT TO DO IN AN EARTHQUAKE

Stay indoors. Stand away from windows,
mirrors and other glass.

Take shelter under a table or desk. This will protect you
from falling objects and give you breathing space. Otherwise,
standing in the corner of a room or in a doorframe is safest.

Lower-level floors are safer than higher ones, but getting
in a lift or trying to run downstairs is dangerous.

If you are outside, lie flat on the ground away
from tall trees and buildings.

If you are near the sea, get to higher ground
as a tidal wave may follow the earthquake.

> If you have ten books you could arrange
> them 3,628,800 ways on your shelf.

FILM FACTS

George Lucas originally had trouble getting funding for *Star Wars Episode IV: A New Hope* because most studios thought that people wouldn't bother going to see it. In fact, it won six Academy Awards, was an enormous box-office hit and is still popular today.

The MGM Studio's lion, Leo, has been played by a number of lions, among them animals called Slats, Jackie and Tanner.

The real name of Toto the dog in *The Wizard of Oz* was Terry - her salary was $125 per week. Judy Garland, who played Dorothy, earned $500 per week.

India's movie industry, Bollywood, is the largest in the world and produces over 800 movies a year. Hollywood only produces half that number.

2,380 kg (5,247 lb) of modelling clay was used in the making of *Chicken Run*.

THE AMOUNT OF DNA YOU SHARE WITH ...

An identical twin..100%

Every other person on earth..............................99.9%

Chimpanzees...98.4%

Other animals..90–97%

Fruit flies..44%

Yeast...26%

Weeds..18%

DNA is short for deoxyribonucleic acid – a long and complicated molecule found inside every cell of all living things. It is said to be the 'blueprint' for life, as every aspect of our physical make-up is determined by it.

CLANDESTINE GOVERNMENT ORGANIZATIONS

CIA
Central Intelligence Agency: US organization responsible for coordinating all intelligence activities.

Gestapo
Secret State Police: secret police force in Nazi Germany, 1936–45.

KGB
Committee of State Security: Soviet Russian security police from 1954–91, responsible for counter-intelligence and 'crimes against the state' in the USSR, and espionage abroad.

MI5
British government agency responsible for intelligence and security on British territory. Its proper name, since 1964, is the Security Service.

MI6
British government agency responsible for intelligence and security overseas. Its proper name, since 1964, is the Secret Intelligence Service (SIS).

LIGHT, SOUND AND ELECTRICITY IN ANIMALS

BIOLUMINESCENCE

This is chemically produced light without heat.

Fireflies and glow-worms use it to send out light signals.

Deep-sea angler fish use it to lure their prey to within gobbling distance.

ECHOLOCATION

Whales and dolphins use a form of sonar that allows them to locate the presence of objects by directing sounds (usually a clicking) towards objects, and interpreting the sound waves that bounce back.

Bats navigate by sending out very high-frequency squeaks, called 'ultrasounds', which are reflected off surfaces as echoes.

ELECTRICITY

The electric eel, which is not an eel at all but a fish that is mostly tail, has a body that acts like a battery. The tail end has a positive charge, and the head region a negative charge. When it touches both its head and tail to another beast it sends a strong electric current – 500–650 volts – through the creature, which is enough to stun or kill prey and to ward off predators.

RADAR

The flat disc of feathers that gives certain owls their distinctive face works like a radar dish, catching sounds and directing them to the owl's ears.

THE MEANING OF DREAMS

Dogs	You will make some new friends.
Kittens	A new phase of your life is about to start.
Ears	You should pay close attention to what is being said to you.
Medals	You will be rewarded.
Falling	You are afraid you are going to be in trouble.
Spies	You are feeling guilty.
Guns	You are frightened of something that is going on in your life.
Bird poo on your head	You should spend less time on your appearance.
Butterflies	Someone is going to give you a present.
Balloons	You are especially happy at the moment.
Delicious food	You will soon be rich.
Swords	One of your friends will soon betray you.
Mazes	You are feeling lost.

STRANGE SWALLOWINGS

Strange objects children have swallowed:
Coins, nappy pins, marbles, rings, batteries, toy parts.

Strange objects adults have swallowed:
False teeth, cutlery, golf balls, toothpicks, screws.

THINGS THAT HAVE CLAWS

Sloths • Lions • Nail hammers • Tigers • Eagles • Mice • Bears
Squirrels • Vultures • Rats • Koalas • Pangolins • Crabs

FIRE TALK

Fireball	A ball-shaped bolt of lightning.
Backdraught	The explosion that occurs when air gets into a space where a fire has died out due to lack of oxygen.
Top fire	Fire that spreads from tree-top to tree-top. It can travel at up to 160 kph (99.4 mph).
Crawling fire	Fire that spreads at ground level.
Jumping fire	Fire that is spread by burning leaves and branches.

The Great Fire of London, which started on 2 September 1666 in a bakery in Pudding Lane, raged for four days and destroyed over 13,000 houses. Amazingly, only six people died. The Bakers' Guild was granted formal forgiveness in 1996.

—— KING ARTHUR'S KNIGHTS OF THE ROUND TABLE ——

Sir Kay • Sir Gareth • Sir Lancelot • Sir Galahad
Sir Bedivere • Sir Gawain • Sir Tristan • Sir Ector • Sir Lionel
Sir Percival • Sir Bors • Sir Tarquin • Sir Mordred

—— NAMES CELEBRITIES HAVE GIVEN THEIR CHILDREN ——

David and Victoria Beckham..Harper

Gwyneth Paltrow and Chris Martin...Apple

Beyoncé and Jay-Z...Blue Ivy

Tom Cruise and Katie Holmes...Suri

Kim Kardashian and Kanye West..North

Nicole Kidman and Keith Urban...Sunday

Jessica Alba and Cash Warren..Haven

Megan Fox and Brian Austin Green....................................Bodhi Ransom

Gwen Stefani and Gavin Rossdale..Apollo

Nicole Richie and Joel Madden...Sparrow

CHOCOLATE TIMELINE

1500–400 BC	The Olmec Indians are the first to grow cocoa trees as a crop.
AD 600	Mayan Indians establish earliest known cocoa plantations in the Yucatán Peninsula, Mexico. They crush the beans into a paste and add spices to make a refreshing and nourishing drink (although it would have been very bitter).
1200s	Aztecs see the tree as a source of strength and wealth, and use the beans as money. They assign their god, Quetzalcóatl, as the tree's guardian.
1500s	European explorers bring the drink back from their travels. Once sweetened, chocolate soon became the fashionable luxury drink.
1847	First ever chocolate bar produced by the British company Fry & Sons.
1861	Richard Cadbury creates the first known heart-shaped chocolate box for Valentine's Day.
1980	An apprentice of the Swiss company Suchard-Tobler tries unsuccessfully to sell secret chocolate recipes to Russia, China and Saudi Arabia.
2005	The whole world is chocolate crazy! In the USA, chocolate consumption is over 5 kg per person per year – that's about 66.5 regular-sized chocolate bars. In Western Europe the average is 8 kg per person – about 106.5 bars. The Swiss are the biggest chocolate eaters, eating 10–12 kg (133–160 bars!) per person each year.
2011	A chocolate egg is sold at auction for £7,000! It is the most expensive non-jewelled egg ever sold and weighs over 50 kg.

FUNNY FACIAL HAIRSTYLES

Muttonchops

Friendly
muttonchops

Handlebar

Bull

Santa

Chin curtain

Anchor

Walrus

Freestyle

Goatee

THREE CUPS TRICK

1. Place three cups upright on a table.

2. Turn the middle cup over so that it is upside-down.

3. Tell your friend that the object of the game is to get all three cups facing downwards in just three moves, but you must turn over two cups at a time.

    Move 1: turn over the middle and left cup

    Move 2: flip the two end cups

    Move 3: turn over the two upright cups

4. You have succeeded. Now turn the middle cup back over LEAVING THE OUTSIDE CUPS FACE DOWN and ask your friend to try.

5. It is impossible. Your friend has started with the cups in the wrong positions, but probably hasn't noticed!

ITEMS NOT ALLOWED IN YOUR HAND LUGGAGE

Ice picks	Pool cues	Dynamite
Knives	Toy guns	Fireworks
Meat cleavers	Guns	Aerosols
Swords	Screwdrivers	Lighters
Baseball bats	Axes	Strike-anywhere matches
Bows and arrows	Saws	
Cricket bats	Drills	Scissors with metal pointed tips
Golf clubs	Cattle prods	

Lord Oxford was so embarrassed when he farted in front of Queen Elizabeth I that he exiled himself for seven years. When he returned the Queen's first words to him were 'My lord, I had forgot the fart.'

————— **EXTREME EARTH** —————

Highest peak	Mount Everest, Himalayas, Nepal-Tibet border, 8,848 m (29,029 ft).
Lowest water surface	The Dead Sea, Israel-Jordan, 413 m (1,356 ft) below sea level.
Highest body of water	Lake Titicaca, Bolivia and Peru, 3,810 m (12,500 ft) above sea level.
Deepest point	Challenger Deep, Mariana Trench, Pacific Ocean, 10,994 m (36,070 ft) deep.
Tallest waterfall	Angel Falls, Venezuela, dropping 979 m (3,212 ft).
Longest river	The Nile, Egypt, 6,695 km (4,160 miles) long.
Largest coral reef	Great Barrier Reef, Australia, spanning 344,400 km^2 (133,000 miles^2) in area.
Greatest river	The Amazon, South America, 6,400 km (4,000 miles) long, drains twice as much land as the Nile.

————— **SKIN DEEP** —————

Average weight of a person's skin.................................2.5 kg (5.5 lb)

Average surface area.................1.5 square metres (16 square ft)

Thinnest...Eyelids (0.5 mm/0.02 in)

Thickest.................................Soles of feet (5 mm/0.2 in)

Weight shed per day...2 g (0.07 oz)

Weight shed in a lifetime...50.8 kg (112 lb)

MYTHICAL CREATURES

BUNYIP
Monstrous, hippo-like
animal that lives in the
watery Australian outback.

GRIFFIN
Legendary creature with
the head, beak and wings
of an eagle and the body
and legs of a lion.

TARASQUE
Monster with six
bear-like legs, an ox-like
body covered with a turtle
shell, a scaly tail ending
in a scorpion's sting,
a lion's head, horse's
ears and the face of
a bitter old man.

KRAKEN
A mile-and-a-half-long,
squid-like sea monster.

NIDHOGG
Serpent-like monster
that eats corpses.

HIPPOCAMPUS
A beast that is half horse
and half fish, with a
serpent's tail.

SPHINX
Monster with the head
of a woman, body of a
lion and wings of a bird.

PHOENIX
Firebird that combusts
and is reborn from
the ashes.

ROC
A huge bird so powerful
it could carry an elephant
to its nest and devour it.

RIDDLES

What common English word will describe a person or thing as not being found in any place, and yet with no changes other than a space between two letters, will correctly describe that person or thing as being actually present at this very moment?

(Nowhere - Now here)

Pete likes beets but not spinach. He likes apples but not pears. He likes jeeps but not vans. He likes Sally but not Sarah. Who will he like - Jimmy or Joe?

(Jimmy - double letters)

Anna has the same number of brothers as she has sisters, but her brother Nat has twice as many sisters as he has brothers. How many boys and how many girls are there in the family?

(4 girls, 3 boys)

Two dogs are sitting on a porch - a fat dog and a thin dog. The thin dog is the son of the fat dog, but the fat dog is not the father of the thin dog. How can this be?

(The fat dog is the thin dog's mother)

MICRO OR NANO?

MICROMETRE (μm)
One millionth of a metre ($1/_{1,000,000}$ m).

A human hair is 100 μm thick.

A bacterium is 1 μm wide.

NANOMETRE (nm)
One-thousand-millionth of a metre ($1/_{1,000,000,000}$ m).
A common-cold virus is 100 nm wide
(i.e. one-tenth the size of a bacterium).

An atom is $1/_{10}$ nm across.

REAL-LIFE PIRATES

Grace O'Malley (Gráinne ni Mháille),
'Pirate Queen of Connacht', 1530-1603

Sir Henry Morgan, 1635-1688

William Kidd, 'Captain Kidd', 1645-1701

William Dampier (famed as an explorer), 1652-1715

Samuel Bellamy, 'Black Bellamy', d.1717

Jack Rackham, 'Calico Jack', d.1720

Edward Teach, 'Blackbeard', 1680-1718

Anne Bonney, 1697/8-1720

Mary Read, d.1721

Jean Laffite, c.1780-c.1826

WHAT DO TOOTHLESS ANIMALS EAT?

Blue whale...Krill (tiny shrimp-like creatures)

Tortoise...Tears off leaves with its horny beak

Anteater...Scoops up ants and other insects with
its long tongue

Pangolin...Eats termites, uses stones and sand
to help break down food

I INVENTED IT. NO, I INVENTED IT

THE TELEPHONE
The German physicist, Johann Philipp Reis, who in 1861
produced a device called the 'Telephon', which transmitted
electrical tones through wires, OR
Scottish-born American Alexander Graham Bell, in 1876, OR
the American Elisha Gray, who may have
just beaten Bell to the post?

THE ZIP (OR ZIPPER)
Elias Howe in 1851, with his 'Automatic, Continuous
Clothing Closure', OR
Whitcomb Judson with his 'Clasp Locker' in 1893, OR
Swedish-born Canadian Gideon Sundback, with his
'Separable Fastener' in 1917?

THE LIGHT BULB
Heinrich Göbel in 1854 - he later won a court
case against Thomas Edison, OR
Joseph Wilson Swan in Britain in 1878, OR
Thomas Edison in 1879?

WHAT YELLOW MEANS

Warning • Warmth • Happiness • Glory • Mourning • Activity
Creativity • Illness • Jealousy • Cowardice • Courage

HOW TO WRITE A HAIKU

A haiku (from the Japanese haikai no ku, meaning 'light verse') is a classical three-line Japanese verse form that follows the pattern below. Traditionally, a haiku is about nature, but you can write yours about whatever you like.

LINE	SYLLABLES	SUGGESTED CONTENT
1	5	The subject of the haiku
2	7	What the subject does
3	5	A summarizing punchline

Example One:
Sunlight on water
Dapples the riverbed where
Hides the spotted trout.

Example Two:
Black-and-white mayhem
Bounces among the branches,
Hungry for baubles.

EXCUSE ME

Chinese...'Dui bu qui'

Croatian...'Oprostite'

Dutch...'Pardon'

French...'Pardonnez-moi'

German..'Entschuldigung'

Greek...'Me synchoreite'

Iranian (Persian/Farsi).......................'Bebakhshid'

Italian...'Scusi'

Japanese...'Sumimasen'

Polish..'Przepraszam'

Russian and Serbian.........................'Izvinite'

Spanish...'Perdón'

Swedish...'Ursäkta'

Yiddish..'Antshuldik(t)'

INCREDIBLE INSECTS

Smallest...Fairyfly wasp, wingspan 0.2 mm (0.008 in)

Largest.........................White Birdwing butterfly, wingspan 30.5 mm (12 in)

Longest................................Giant stick insect, total length 50 cm (20 in)

Heaviest.......................................Goliath beetle, weight 100 gm (3.5 oz)

Loudest.................Cicada, can be heard from 400 m (0.25 miles) away

Most beautiful..Madagascan sunset moth

Best jumper.......................Flea, can jump 150 times its own body length

Fastest flyer...Dragonfly, 56 kph (35 mph)

Longest living...........................Queen of termites, lives 50-100 years

Most dangerous...................Australian bulldog ant, sting can kill humans

Most social.................Ants, work together in highly organized colonies

Most annoying...Tiny biting midge

The oldest playable musical instrument is a flute that was discovered in an ancient burial site in China. It is over 9,000 years old and is carved from a bird's wing bone. It can still be played, making a high reedy sound, not unlike a penny whistle.

YY U R YY U B I C U R YY 4 ME

Too wise you are, too wise you be,
I see you are too wise for me.

FAMOUS NOBEL PRIZE WINNERS

Marie Curie	Physics (research into radioactivity), 1903, and Chemistry (discovery of radium and polonium), 1911
Theodore Roosevelt	Peace (collaboration of various peace treaties), 1906
Rudyard Kipling	Literature (novels, poems and short stories including *The Jungle Book*), 1907
Albert Einstein	Physics (discovery of the law of the photoelectric effect), 1921
Thomas Stearns Eliot	Literature (outstanding contribution to poetry), 1948
John Steinbeck	Literature (novels including *The Grapes of Wrath* and *Of Mice and Men*), 1962
Martin Luther King	Peace (leader of the 'Southern Christian Leadership Conference'), 1964
Mother Teresa	Peace (leader of 'Missionaries of Charity'), 1979
Nelson Mandela	Peace (peaceful termination of the apartheid regime in South Africa), 1993
Barack H. Obama	Peace (efforts to strengthen international diplomacy and cooperation), 2009

REAL ALTERNATIVES TO TOILET PAPER

Water • Hands • Newspapers or magazines

Leaves • Stones • Shells • Feathers • Corn cobs • Rope

Sticks • Sand • Rags • Wet sponge • Money

HOW MANY MAGPIES?

One for sorrow,

Two for joy,

Three for a girl,

And four for a boy,

Five for silver,

Six for gold,

Seven for a secret never to be told.

MESSAGE NOT ALWAYS FULLY UNDERSTOOD

Your nerves send messages to the brain, but their messages are not always that accurate. Try this experiment with a friend.

1. Have one arm bare to the elbow. Shut your eyes and keep them shut.

2. Ask your friend to tap the inside of your forearm gently with a fingertip. He or she should start at the wrist, then progress slowly up towards your elbow.

3. When you think your friend has reached the crease on the inside of your elbow tell your friend to stop and open your eyes.

4. Has your friend's finger reached the inside of your elbow, or has your brain misunderstood the message?

Farts are made up of five different gases, mainly nitrogen. The smell comes from substances in your poo called skatole and indole (ironically both are used in the manufacture of perfumes).

SIEGE ENGINES

BALLISTA
A machine like a giant crossbow that used wound-up ropes to fire a projectile (usually a rock) straight and low.

SPRING ENGINE
Similar to a ballista, but used spring arms of metal or horn to fire a heavy iron dart, like a giant crossbow bolt.

TREBUCHET
Used a counterweight at the end of a long pivoted arm to fling very large (up to half a tonne) boulders and other projectiles, including balls of flaming pitch and the heads of captured enemies, high in the air for considerable distances.

TRACTION CATAPULT
Worked like a trebuchet, but used human power (usually several soldiers heaving together), instead of a counterweight, to pull down one end of a long pivoted arm to release the projectile in a sling at the other end.

ONAGER
Meaning 'wild donkey', probably because it 'kicked' like one. This was like a cross between a ballista and a trebuchet, and used wound-up ropes to propel a catapult arm, hurling a projectile from a cup at the long end of the arm.

STRANGE REMEDIES

EYE DISEASES
Bathe eyes with rainwater collected before dawn in June.

Apply a mixture of tortoise brain and honey to your eye.

Rub with the tail of a black cat.

Dab with a few drops of urine.

TOOTHACHE
Press a new nail into the gum and aching tooth until it bleeds, then hammer the nail into a tree.

Burn one ear with a hot poker.

Tie a dead mole around your neck.

DIARRHOEA
Eat Ggruel, green onions, oil, honey, wax and water, or coca leaves.

COMMON COLD
Put mustard and onions up your nose.

Tie a sweaty sock around your neck.

WARTS
Dab with dog's pee.

Spread pig's blood on them.

Daub with mashed-up slugs.

Stroke with a tortoiseshell cat's tail in the month of May.

Dribble over the warts first thing in the morning.

HEADACHE
Drill a hole in your skull.

Rub cow dung on the temples.

Lean head against a tree while someone drives a nail into the opposite side of the trunk.

Tie the head of a buzzard round your neck.

Sleep with a pair of 'pain-cutting' scissors under the pillow.

GOITRE AND TUMOURS
Touch with a hanged man's hand.

THINGS THAT HARM THE PLANET

Burning fossil fuels

Cars and aeroplanes

Wasting things

Leaving on the TV/lights/heating/electricity

Leaving hosepipes or taps on

Dumping rubbish/littering

GOOD LUCK

Stroking a black cat.

Finding a four-leaf clover.

Hanging a horseshoe
above a door.

Carrying a hare's foot.

Finding a coin heads-up.

Wearing new clothes at Easter.

Seeing a chimney sweep.

Finding a frog or cricket
in the house.

BAD LUCK

Seeing three butterflies
together.

Letting milk boil over.

Stepping on a crack
in the pavement.

Walking under a ladder.

Breaking a mirror.

Opening an umbrella indoors.

Leaving a house through
a different door than the one
through which you entered.

THINGS THAT SHRINK

Icebergs • Old people

SPORTING LOSERS

BOXING
Daniel Caruso was so enthusiastic warming up for the Golden Gloves Championships in 1992 that he punched himself in the face and broke his nose. Doctors decided he was unfit to fight.

MARATHON RUNNING
Leda Diaz de Cano was so far behind the other competitors in the 1984 Olympics that officials had to persuade her to give up so they could reopen the streets to traffic.

MOTORCYCLING
While waving to the crowd after finishing fourth in the 500cc US Motorcycle Championship in 1989, Kevin Magee fell off his bike and broke his leg.

RUGBY
A team from Doncaster, UK, lost 40 games in a row. On one occasion the players failed to recognize their own strip because they were covered in mud, and began to tackle members of their own team.

FOOTBALL
Rio Ferdinand, one of the world's most expensive defenders, strained a tendon in his knee, not while he was playing or in training, but by leaving his foot up on the coffee table while watching television.

THE WORST PLACE TO ...

Eat a hamburger.............................On a roller coaster

Fall over.............................In a stinging-nettle patch

Fart.............................In the headmaster's office

Cut yourself.............................In a river full of piranhas

Skateboard.............................On gravel

Have a giggling fit.............................In assembly

Bang yourself.............................On your funny bone

Be sick.............................In a tent

THE RHYMING WEATHER FORECAST

Red sky at morning, sailors take warning.
Red sky at night, sailors' delight.

When the dew is on the grass, rain will never come to pass.

Ring around the moon, rain by noon.
Ring around the sun, rain before night is done.

Rain before seven, fine before eleven.

A cow with its tail to the west makes the weather best,
A cow with its tail to the east makes the weather least.

If the oak is out before the ash then we are in for a splash.
But if the ash is out before the oak we are in for a soak.

The rain, it raineth on the just
And also on the unjust fella:
But chiefly on the just, because
The unjust steals the just's umbrella.

THINGS WE USE TREES FOR

Oxygen

Shade

Fuel

Buildings

Furniture

Musical instruments

Reducing noise pollution

Lowering air temperature

Vital drugs

Paper

Rubber

Building blocks

Homes for birds

Tree houses

SHAKESPEAREAN INSULTS

'Your bum is the greatest thing about you.'
Measure for Measure

'Pray you, stand farther away from me.'
Antony and Cleopatra

'Thou art a boil, a plague-sore, an embossed carbuncle.'
King Lear

'You Banbury cheese!'
The Merry Wives of Windsor

'Thy food is such as hath been belched on by infected lungs.'
Pericles, Prince of Tyre

'Were I like thee, I'd throw away myself.'
Timon of Athens

ABBREVIATIONS

AKA...Also Known As

ASAP...As Soon As Possible

DVD..Digital Versatile Disk

ETA..Estimated Time of Arrival

ISP..Internet Service Provider

LOL...Laugh Out Loud

NB...Nota Bene (note well)

RSVP............................Répondez S'il Vous Plaît (please reply)

TARDIS.........................Time And Relative Dimension In Space

FIFO..First In First Out

AWOL...Absent Without Leave

BYO...Bring Your Own

TBC..To Be Confirmed

SWAT.....................................Special Weapons and Tactics

SCUBA....Self-Contained Underwater Breathing Apparatus

FAMOUS REAL-LIFE DOGS

Pickles, the dog who found the stolen Football World Cup in 1966.

Strelka and Belka, who returned safely to earth after a day in space in 1960.

Barry, a St. Bernard who rescued over 40 people stranded in the Alps.

Rico, a Border collie who understands over 200 words.

FAMOUS REAL-LIFE CATS

Sugar, the cat who walked some 1,500 miles across the USA to rejoin her owners, who had given her away when they moved.

Scarlett, who rescued her five kittens from a burning building in New York in 1996.

Solomon, the white chinchilla longhair who played Blofeld's cat in the James Bond films.

MYSTERIOUS MONSTERS

BIGFOOT - Movie footage captured a large, hairy creature in a Californian forest. Some experts say it is a direct descendant of a kind of giant ape that once lived in China. Bigfoot is described as standing 2-3 m (7-10 ft) tall and weighing over 225 kg (500 lb), with footprints 43 cm (17 in) long.

NESSIE - People have reported seeing a mysterious creature in Loch Ness, a lake in Scotland. Despite several alleged sightings, Nessie has never been found. The monster may be a sturgeon, a fish with a long snout and bony lumps on its back. Sturgeon can grow to 6 m (20 ft) long.

STORSIE - People claim to have seen a mystery sea monster in Lake Storsjön, Sweden. Some say the beast has a head like a horse; others say it's a big, worm-like serpent. Accounts agree that the creature has large eyes, an enormous mouth, and is between 9 and 12 m (30 and 40 ft) in length.

MOKELE-MBEMBE - From the jungles of Africa have come many reported sightings of a strange beast known as Mokele-Mbembe. Described as an animal with a long neck and tail, and round-shaped feet with three claws, it has all the characteristics of a sauropod dinosaur!

YETI - A mysterious creature said to live in the Himalayan Mountains of Asia. It is reported to be big, ape-like, hairy and smelly. Some people call it the Abominable Snowman, others call it Yeti, which means 'big eater'.

MAZES OF THE WORLD

Roman maze

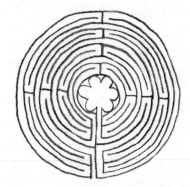

Medieval maze at
Chartres, France

Ancient Greek maze
from Crete

Hampton Court maze in
London, UK - the world's
oldest hedge maze

LOST IN A MAZE

A unicursal maze has only one path to follow, and
while it may feel like you are getting lost as you
twist and turn, you will eventually reach the goal.

A multicursal maze has branches and forks
that require you to guess the correct path.

If lost, apply the 'right-hand rule'. Keep your
right hand against the maze wall as you walk.
You are guaranteed a way out - eventually.

VITAMIN DEFICIENCIES

VITAMIN AND WHERE TO FIND IT	SYMPTOMS OF DEFICIENCY
Vitamin A (carrots, cabbage)	Scaly skin, poor growth
Vitamin B1 (thiamine) (peas, beans, grains)	Beriberi: loss of appetite, tiredness, aching joints, numbness in hands and feet, heart problems
Vitamin B2 (riboflavin) (cereal, milk)	Poor digestion, eye disorders, dry and flaky skin, sore red tongue
Vitamin B3 (niacin) (chicken, tuna)	Pellagra: weakness, skin inflammation, diarrhoea, weight loss, depression, confusion, memory loss
Vitamin B6 (pyridoxine) (beans, fish)	Depression, nausea, weakness, greasy and flaky skin
Vitamin B7 or H (biotin) (spinach)	Heart abnormalities, appetite (eggs, loss, fatigue, depression, dry skin
Vitamin B12 (beef, shellfish)	Anaemia, fatigue, nerve damage, smooth tongue, very sensitive skin
Vitamin C (oranges, strawberries)	Scurvy: tiredness, aching, sores that won't heal, swollen gums, teeth fall out
Vitamin D (salmon, eggs)	Rickets: deformed skull, curved spine, bowed legs, knobbly growths on ends of bones
Vitamin E (green leafy veg)	Nervous-system problems
Vitamin K (broccoli, cheese)	Thin blood, danger of bleeding to death

---

Ask a friend to think of a word that rhymes with orange, purple or silver.

TOP FIVE ALL-TIME WORLDWIDE BOX-OFFICE HITS

ONE
Avatar (2009)

TWO
Titanic (1997)

THREE
The Avengers (2012)

FOUR
Harry Potter and the Deathly Hallows: Part 2 (2011)

FIVE
Frozen (2013)

THE CHINESE CALENDAR

2010...Tiger

2011...Rabbit

2012...Dragon

2013...Snake

2014...Horse

2015...Goat

2016...Monkey

2017...Rooster

2018...Dog

2019...Pig

2020...Rat

2021...Ox

And then back to tiger – it is a 12-year cycle.

PHRENOLOGY

According to phrenology, the many aspects of a person's character can be seen in 'bumps' on the surface of the brain. The skull follows the shape of the brain and shows these bumps. As the personality developed so would the bumps – those corresponding to much-used characteristics growing and those corresponding to little-used characteristics shrinking. These bumps could change with character over time. The diagram below shows which bumps relate to which characteristics.

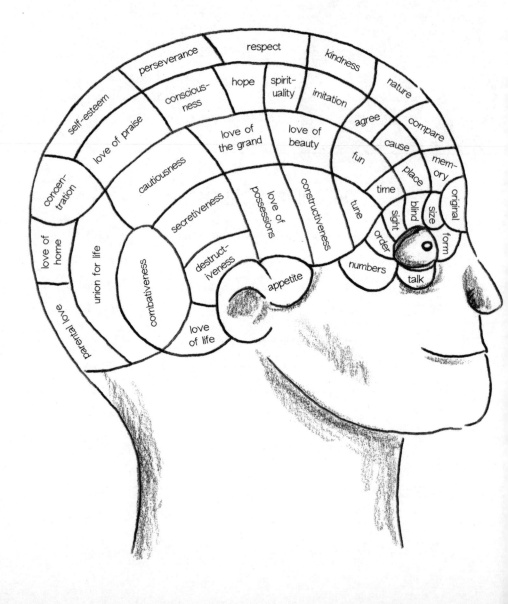

CAUSES OF CROP-CIRCLES: THEORIES

Landscape artists • Evil entities • Aliens
Freak whirlwinds • Unknown natural energies
Hoaxers • Intelligent balls of white light

BODY APPENDAGES

CLAY LIP PLATES (Mursi people, Omo Valley, Ethiopia)
When a Mursi girl reaches the age of 15 or 16, her bottom lip is pierced and a clay lip plate is inserted. As the lip stretches, larger and larger plates are inserted. It is thought that the larger the lip plate, the greater the number of cattle required in exchange for her hand in marriage.

BRASS NECK RINGS (Padaung tribe, Burma)
As young girls, women from the Padaung tribe are given brass rings to wear around their necks. As they grow up, more and more rings are added and this gives them the appearance of having extraordinarily long necks. In fact, the rings do not stretch the neck, but rather the weight of them pushes down on the collarbone until it appears to be a part of the neck.

EARLOBE PIERCINGS (global)
In Western culture it is common for men and women to pierce their ears. Sometimes, by gradually increasing the size of the part of the ring that goes through the piercing, people increase the size of the holes to accommodate large earplugs.

ANIMALS THAT CAN CHANGE COLOUR

Chameleon • Flounder • Octopus • Cuttlefish
Golden tortoise beetle • Bark spider

SPACE FIRSTS

FIRST SATELLITE
The Soviet Russian Sputnik 1,
launched into orbit around the
earth on 4 October 1957.

FIRST ANIMAL IN SPACE
Laika, a dog, on board the
Soviet Russian Sputnik 2 on
3 November 1957.

FIRST MAN IN SPACE
Soviet Russian cosmonaut
Yuri Gagarin, aboard Vostok
1 on 12 April 1961.

FIRST WOMAN IN SPACE
Soviet Russian cosmonaut
Valentina Tereshkova, who
piloted Vostok 6 in orbit
around the earth for four
days in 1963.

FIRST SPACE WALK
Soviet Russian Aleksei A.
Leonov, on 18 March 1965, left
the Voskhod 2 spacecraft and
floated tethered in space for
12 minutes.

FIRST SPACE STATION
Soviet Russia's Salyut 1,
launched in April 1971.

FIRST SPACE SHUTTLE
America's Columbia, launched
on 12 April 1981.

FIRST MOON LANDING
Soviet Russia's Luna 9,
launched 31 January 1966.

FIRST MOON WALK
American astronaut
Neil Armstrong, commander
of the Apollo 11 lunar
mission, walked on the
moon on 20 July 1969.

FIRST WORDS SPOKEN
ON THE MOON
'Tranquility Base here.
The Eagle has landed ...
OK, Houston, I'm on the
porch ... I'm at the foot
of the ladder. The LEM
footpads are on the, uh,
depressed in the surface about
one or two inches. Going to
step off the LEM now. That's
one small step for [a] man,
one giant leap for mankind.'
Neil Armstrong on
20 July 1969.

ARE YOU IN PROPORTION?

Fingertip to wrist = Hairline to chin

Big toe to heel = Elbow to wrist

Outstretched fingertip to outstretched fingertip = Head to toe

Knee to ankle = Elbow to fingertip

ONOMATOPOEIC WORDS

(Words that sound like what they refer to.)

SPLASH	SQUEAK	HUSH	GRUNT
WHINE	CRACKLE	CHIME	HISS
THUD	BABBLE	BOOM	POP
CLANG	TINKLE	PING-PONG	HOOT
PURR	MOAN	WHIRR	GONG

THE GREAT PYRAMID OF KHUFU (OR CHEOPS) AT GIZA

Built: 2589-2566 BC

Purpose: Pharaoh Khufu's burial chamber

Time to build: 20 years

Number of labourers: 20,000-30,000

Machinery used: Elementary 'cranes', manpower, scaffolding, ropes of papyrus twine, ramps of stone, wood and mud

Weight: 6 million tonnes

Number of 'bricks' (granite and limestone blocks): 2,300,000

Height on completion: 146.5 m (481 ft)

Height now: 137 m (449 ft)

Amazing fact: It was the tallest building in the world until the early 20th century - some 45 centuries!

THE ENIGMA MACHINE

The Enigma machine was a portable electrical and mechanical device for encoding and decoding messages. Invented by the German, Arthur Scherbius in 1918, it was housed in a wooden case and resembled an old-fashioned typewriter keyboard, with a set of removable and interchangeable wheels (rotors) towards the back, and letter keys at the front.

By the Second World War, the machine had been adopted by the German armed forces and modified to suit their needs, then produced in large quantities. The Germans unquestioningly believed that the Allies would never be able to break the machine's codes as there were so many thousands of possibilities. There was one weak spot, though: the day's settings for a machine had to be sent between encoder and decoder, and these settings were often captured by the Allies. One of the machines was intercepted in Poland and smuggled to Britain. Then, with the help of some Polish mathematicians, cryptologists based in Buckinghamshire, UK, succeeded in breaking the codes of a large number of intercepted Nazi messages, and gained vital military intelligence from them.

WHAT RED MEANS

Stop • Danger • Emergency • Love • Passion
Hatred • Anger • Power • Energy • Importance • Luck
Success • Happiness • Prosperity

WHO IS THAT CELEBRITY?

Bruno Mars...Peter Gene Hernandez

Calvin Harris...Adam Richard Wiles

Elton John...Reginald Kenneth Dwight

Eminem...Marshall Bruce Mathers

Iggy Azalea...Amethyst Amelia Kelly

Jamie Foxx..Eric Marlon Bishop

Jennifer Aniston...Jennifer Linn Anastassakis

Lady Gaga.......................................Stefani Joanne Angelina Germanotta

Lana Del Rey...Elizabeth Grant

P!nk...Alecia Moore

> The first number (written out)
> to have the letter 'a' in it is
> 'one hundred and one'.

SURVIVORS OF ASSASSINATION ATTEMPTS

Elizabeth I, Queen of England (1570)

Napoleon I, Emperor of France (1809)

Theodore Roosevelt, President of the USA (1912)

Adolf Hitler, German dictator (1944)

Andy Warhol, American artist (1968)

Bob Marley, Jamaican reggae singer (1976)

Pope John Paul II (1981 and 1995)

Margaret Thatcher, British Prime Minister (1984)

Jacques Chirac, President of France (2002)

Queen Beatrix and her family, Queen of the Netherlands (2009)

——————— AN ALCHEMIST'S RECIPE FOR GOLD ———————

An Alchemist's Recipe for Gold

PART 1:

Agents

> 454 g (1 lb) vitriol, 454 g (1 lb) sal ammoniac, 454 g (1 lb)
> arinat, 454 g (1 lb) sal nitrate, 454 g (1 lb) sal gemmae, 454 g
> (1 lb) alumen crudum, ground antimony ore (antimonium).

Method

> Mix all the agents apart from the antimonium thoroughly.
> Place in a conical flask over a bunsen burner, and distil to
> form a water-like substance. Dissolve the antimonium in this
> substance and leave until solid deposits are formed. Remove
> these solids and wash them.

PART 2:

Agents

> Antimonium, distilled vinegar

Method

> Put the antimonium in a vial and pour in the distilled vinegar.
> Place the vial in a pan of hot water, and leave for 40 days.
> You will now have a red liquid. Pour this liquid into a flask
> and mix with some more distilled vinegar. Distil the solution
> to create a dry powder.

PART 3:

Agents

> Distilled water, spirit wine.

Method

> Wash the powder from part 2 with the distilled water, and
> leave to dry. The antimonium will now be bright red in
> colour. Place the antimonium in a vial, add the spirit wine,
> and place the vial in a pan of warm water for four days.

Repeat this process of distillation and refinement until you have
gold (note: you won't have actual gold, just a gold-looking metal).

'FACTS' THAT ARE NOT TRUE

Chewing gum takes seven years to pass through the human digestive system, if it doesn't kill you first.

The word 'nylon' is from New York and London.

The bra was invented by Otto Titzling.

There are alligators living in New York City's sewers.

The French queen Marie Antoinette said 'Let them eat cake' when she heard that the country's poor had no bread.

No two snowflakes are alike.

Elephants are afraid of mice.

ANIMALS THAT METAMORPHOSE

Frogspawn	Tadpole	Froglet	Frog
Egg	Caterpillar	Chrysalis	Butterfly
Egg	Caterpillar	Cocoon	Moth
Egg	Maggot	Pupa	Fly
Egg	Grub	Pupa	Beetle
Egg	Larva	Nymph	Dragonfly

STACK THE BLOCKS

WHAT DO YOU GET WHEN YOU CROSS ...

A vampire and a snowman?...Frostbite

A sheep and a kangaroo?............................A woolly jumper

A centipede and a parrot?............................A walkie-talkie

A karate expert and a pig?............................A pork chop

A fish and an elephant?............................Swimming trunks

A cat and a duck?............................A duck-filled fatty puss

A beetle and a rabbit?............................Bugs Bunny

Rudolph and a weatherman?............................Rain, dear

A frog and a traffic warden?............................Toad away

A computer and a potato?............................Microchips

A flea and some moon rock?............................A lunar-tick

A dessert and an aircraft?............................A jelly copter

A monster and a chicken?............................Free strange eggs

GREAT WARRIORS

HANNIBAL
247–182 BC – Carthaginian general who marched a huge army (including 40 elephants) across the Alps from Spain to attack Rome. Many years later he killed himself rather than surrender to the Romans.

TAMERLANE
1336–1405 – Mongol emperor who was partially paralysed on his left side. He conquered a huge area stretching from the Mediterranean to western India and all the way up to Russia. He was extremely cruel to his enemies and built pyramids of skulls every time he destroyed a city.

ALEXANDER THE GREAT
356–323 BC – King of Macedonia. He was taught by the philosopher Aristotle and could tame wild horses. He became king aged 20 and managed to crush a Greek rebellion, conquer Persia, Egypt and part of India, all before he died at the age of 33.

ATTILA THE HUN
406–453 BC – Killed his brother to become king and is said to have eaten two of his children. Formed a huge army and destroyed many cities in the Roman Empire. He eventually died of a nosebleed after getting very drunk on his wedding night.

HOW FAST IS THE WORLD SPINNING?

The Earth spins round on an axis that runs from the North to South Pole. This means that the further away you get from the poles, the faster the earth spins.

North and South Pole	0 kph (0 mph)
Iceland	700 kph (345 mph)
United Kingdom	990 kph (615 mph)
Spain	1,200 kph (746 mph)
Central USA	1,200 kph (746 mph)
Australia	1,400 kph (870 mph)
Kenya (equator)	1,600 kph (994 mph)

SILLY SIGNS

In a church: 'A bean supper will be held on Tuesday evening in the church hall. Music will follow.'

In a safari park: 'Elephants please stay in your car.'

At a post office: 'This door is not to be used as an exit or an entrance.'

In a park: 'No cycling dogs on leads.'

On a roadside: 'Animals drive very slowly.'

At a zoo: 'Those who throw objects at the crocodiles will be asked to retrieve them.'

At an optician's: 'If you don't see what you're looking for, you've come to the right place.'

THE NATO PHONETIC ALPHABET

A	Alpha	H	Hotel	O	Oscar	V	Victor
B	Bravo	I	India	P	Papa	W	Whisky
C	Charlie	J	Juliet	Q	Quebec	X	X-Ray
D	Delta	K	Kilo	R	Romeo	Y	Yankee
E	Echo	L	Lima	S	Sierra	Z	Zulu
F	Foxtrot	M	Mike	T	Tango		
G	Golf	N	November	U	Uniform		

CRIMINAL MASTERMINDS?

Two car-radio thieves in Austria were busted when police followed footprints they had left in the snow from car to car, and then to their flat.

Romanian police were questioning a pair of women about a mobile phone reported stolen: when one of the officers dialled the number of the stolen phone, a ringing was heard – from one of the suspects' underpants.

In China, a young burglar broke into an office and filled up his bag with cash and valuables. Then he looked in the fridge and ate the cakes and drank the milk he found there. Feeling tired, he lay down for a bit. Members of staff arriving in the morning found him still there, fast asleep.

In Wales, an armed bank robber waited patiently while the cashier carefully counted and then recounted the money he was to hand over. By the time he had finished counting, very slowly, the police had arrived.

An armed bank robber in Iowa, USA, got his cash and jumped into his getaway car. The vehicle had a personalized registration plate that carried the thief's surname.

In the USA, a police officer tried calling the car phone of a lady whose vehicle had been stolen. When the car thief answered, the officer pretended that he had seen a notice advertising the car for sale and was interested in buying it. Suspecting nothing, the thief made an appointment to meet the officer.

In the USA, a burglar broke into a home and made away with various electronic articles, including a digital camera. Stupidly, he took a photo of himself which he forgot to wipe off the camera before taking it to a pawnshop.

In Japan, an armed burglar broke into what he thought were the offices of Japan Railways and loudly demanded money – to find himself surrounded by police officers. He'd broken into a police dormitory.

SOMETHING FISHY

HAGFISH
A primitive marine fish with a slimy, eel-like body and no proper jaw. It has a slit-like mouth, and feeds off dead or dying fish.

SEA HORSE
A small marine fish with a tube-like snout, segmented bony armour and a curled tail, which swims upright in the water.

COELACANTH
Last surviving relative of a prehistoric group of fishes. It was thought to be long extinct until 1938, when one was captured alive.

PIPE FISH
A long, thin tubular fish resembling a straightened-out seahorse (to which it's related).

LUNGFISH
Has two primitive lungs, allowing it to breathe air so that it can survive out of water and live in mud for long periods during droughts.

PUFFERFISH
Various species of globe-shaped fish with spiny skins; when alarmed or threatened, they can inflate themselves with air or water like a balloon. Can be poisonous.

I FEEL THE NEED, THE NEED FOR SPEED

Speed of light..........1.02 billion kph (669,600,000 mph)

Speed of sound..........1,225 kph (761 mph)

Speed of Concorde..........2,173 kph (1,350 mph)

Land speed record..........1,228 kph (763 mph)

Fastest passenger train..........Japan's Maglev, 603.5 kph (375 mph)

Fastest animal..........Peregrine falcon, 386 kph (240 mph)

Fastest land animal..........Cheetah, 94 kph (58 mph)

Fastest two-legged animal..........Ostrich, 70 kph (43.5 mph)

Fastest human..........Usain Bolt, 44.72 kph (27.79 mph)

Fastest snail..........0.048 kph (0.03 mph)

HOW TO ARRANGE AN ORCHESTRA

A	Conductor	I	Violas
B	First violins	J	Basses
C	Second violins	K	Harp
D	Flutes	L	Percussion
E	Clarinets	M	Horns
F	Bassoons	N	Trombones
G	Oboes	O	Trumpets
H	Cellos	P	Tuba

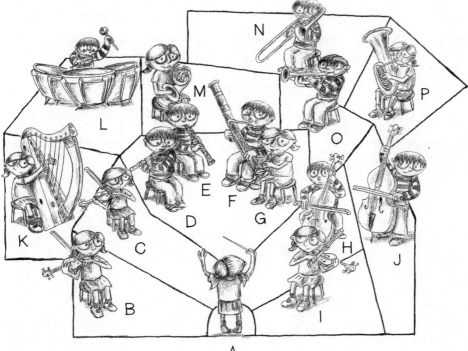

The average four-year-old asks
over 400 questions a day.

THE ORIGINS OF TEXT MESSAGING

1844	First telegraph message: 'What hath God wrought.' (Samuel Morse)
1861	First message on a 'Telephon': 'A horse does not eat a cucumber salad.' (Johann Philipp Reis)
1876	First words transmitted by telephone: 'Mr Watson, come here; I want you.' (Alexander Graham Bell)
1901	First transatlantic radio message, 'click-click-click', meaning 's' in Morse code. (Guglielmo Marconi)
1924	First facsimile (fax) message transmitted across Atlantic, from New York to Sweden.
1949	First message sent by telephone pager. (Al Gross)
1973	First call on a mobile cellphone (by the inventor Martin Cooper to his main rival).
1992	First text message sent.

EMOTICONS

:-)	I'm happy
:-(	I'm sad
;-)	I'm winking
:-D	I'm laughing
:'-(	I'm crying
:'-D	I'm crying with laughter
:-l	I'm bored
:-X	Kiss
:-0	Oops!
:==)	I've got two noses!
:_(	Someone just punched me in the nose
.-(	I've lost a contact lens
>;-)	I've just had an evil thought

REAL NEWSPAPER HEADLINES

Iraqi Head Seeks Arms

Drunk Gets Nine Months in Violin Case

British Left Waffles on Falkland Islands

Two Sisters Reunited after 18 Years in Checkout

War Dims Hope for Peace

Typhoon Rips Through Cemetery: Hundreds Dead

Chef Throws His Heart into Helping Feed Needy

Air Head Fired

Kids Make Nutritious Snacks

Enraged Cow Injures Farmer with Axe

CARTOON CATS

Felix

Tom

Top Cat

Sylvester

Garfield

CARTOON DOGS

Goofy

Pluto

Snoopy

Santa's Little Helper

Scooby Doo

WHO'S THE TALLEST?

Answer: They're all the same size.

REDS, BLUES AND GREENS

Brick	Aquamarine	Apple
Burgundy	Azure	Avocado
Carmine	Cerulean	Beryl
Claret	Cobalt	Chartreuse
Crimson	Cornflower	Emerald
Maroon	Cyan	Fir
Rose madder	Indigo	Leaf
Rouge	Navy	Lime
Ruby	Prussian	Moss
Russet	Robin's-egg	Olive
Rust	Royal	Pine
Scarlet	Sapphire	Sage
Vermilion	Ultramarine	Sea

WAYS TO CHOOSE WHO IS 'IT'

Everyone makes a fist with both hands. You then go round the group touching one fist for each of the words of the rhyme. The fist that the last word lands on is out. The rhyme is repeated until just one fist is left, and that person is 'it'.

'Ip dip sky blue, who's it not you.'

'One potato, two potato, three potato, four, five potato, six potato, seven potato, more - that means you are not it.'

'Ippy dippy dation my operation how many people at the station' - at this point the person whose fist you're on gives a number e.g. three that you then count out - 'one, two, three.'

'Ibble obble black bobble ibble obble out.'

'Dip dip dip, my blue ship, sails on the water, like a cup and saucer - O-U-T spells out.'

WHAT DOES YOUR HANDWRITING SAY ABOUT YOU?

Large letters.....................Flamboyant and outgoing, a bit of a show-off

Small letters.............................Timid and shy with a good eye for detail

Right sloping letters................................Open and honest, likes attention

Left sloping letters...Shy and reserved

Upright letters....................................Fair and always willing to listen

Lines slant upwards..Positive, optimistic

Lines slant downwards............A bit moody, could do with cheering up

Lines slant up and down................................Unpredictable, indecisive

Rounded letters.............................Logical and usually gets things right

Spiky letters...Quick-thinking and perceptive

All capital letters..Trying to hide something

Unusual dots...Artistic and creative

Regular and neat....................Reliable, organized and good in a crisis

Great Britain was the first country to issue postage stamps, which is why they are the only stamps in the world not to bear the name of the country of origin. The first stamp was issued on 1 May 1840 and came to be known as the Penny Black.

THINGS THAT ARE FUN TO SAY

'Eenie-meanie-macka-racka-rare-rar-domi-nacka-chicker-pocker-lolly-popper-om-pom-push'

'Glockenspiel'

'Super-cali-fragi-listic-expi-ali-docious'

'In a tiny house, by a tiny stream, sat a lovely lass, who had a lovely dream, and the dream came true, quite unexpectedly, in a gilly gilly hoser-neffer-kaba-neller-bogen by the sea.'

'Antidisestablishmentarianism'

'Tell me no secrets I'll tell you no lies, I saw a policeman doing up his flies are a nuisance bees are worse, and that is the end of my silly little verse.'

Try inserting your own name where the Xs are in this rhyme:
'Xxxx, Xxxx, bo, bxxx, banana farner fo fxxx, fee, fi mo mxxx, Xxxx.'
So, if your name were 'Jack', you would get:
'Jack, Jack, bo, back, banana farner fo fack, fee, fi, mo, mack, Jack.'

LIKE WHICH ANIMAL?

Canine..Dog

Feline..Cat

Bovine..Cow

Ovine..Sheep

Porcine..Pig

Ursine..Bear

Equine..Horse

Vulpine..Fox

Leporine..Rabbit/hare

Anatine..Duck

Serpentine..Snake

Cervine..Deer

Delphine..Dolphin

Phocine..Seal

Elephantine..Elephant

Musteline.........Weasel, ferret, mink, stoat etc.

INVENTIONS THAT DIDN'T MAKE IT

Thomas Edison's AUTOMATIC VOTE RECORDER (1869) – Politicians didn't like it, perhaps because it was too accurate.

Henry Bessemer's ANTI-SEASICK BOAT (1875) – Sailed straight into the pier at Calais because it could not be steered.

Sarah Guppy's ALL-IN-ONE BREAKFAST URN (1912) – Could boil eggs and keep toast warm while boiling water for tea.

Bill Gates's TRAFF-O-DATA (1974) – Could analyse the information collected by roadside car-counting devices.

Clive Sinclair's SINCLAIR C5 (1985) – A small, three-wheeled vehicle with a plastic body, an electric motor and pedals for extra assistance going up hills.

THE PREDICTIONS OF NOSTRADAMUS

Michel de Notre-Dame (Nostradamus) was a 16th-century French physician and astrologer who claimed to have visions of the future. He wrote a series of four-line verses in which he is believed to have predicted:

The death of King Henry II of France

Louis Pasteur's discovery of germs

The First World War

The rise of Hitler

The suspicious death of Pope John Paul I

The explosion of the space shuttle Challenger

The attacks on the Twin Towers in New York

THREE TERRIFYING PEOPLE

THE CANNIBAL
Hidden in a mile-deep remote cave in 17th-century Scotland, Sawney Beane and his family survived by ambushing travellers, robbing them – then eating them. It was 25 years before they were discovered, and when the horrified authorities found the cave it was filled with stolen jewellery and salted human remains hanging in rows along the cave walls.

THE IMPALER
Vlad Dracula, Prince of Wallachia (1431–1476), was the inspiration for Bram Stoker's novel about a blood-sucking vampire of the same surname. He ruled through terror, and killed tens of thousands of his own people – mainly by publicly impaling them on stakes.

THE BLOOD BATHER
Elizabeth, Countess of Bathory (1560–1614), is said to have tortured and killed up to 2,000 girls and young women in Transylvania. She used a whip with articulated silver claws to tear the victim's flesh. According to legend, she believed that bathing in their blood – and drinking the blood of the prettier ones – would keep her looking young and beautiful.

BIG BIRDS

Three ginormous birds – all flightless and now extinct.

THE ELEPHANT BIRD
Otherwise known as Aepyornis, this huge bird from Madagascar was up to 2.7 m (9 ft) tall, and weighed as much as 450 kg (992 lb). It may have survived until the arrival of the first humans on the island, and have given rise to the legend of the Roc (see p. 43).

'THE GIANT DEMON DUCK OF DOOM'
Dromornis stirtoni from Australia was even bigger, reaching 3 m (9.8 ft), and weighing up to 500 kg (1,102 lb). This is about the same as a large horse.

THE GIANT MOA
This huge bird from New Zealand was possibly the tallest ever to walk the Earth. They reached 4 m (13 ft) in height, which is almost as tall as a double-decker bus.
They were more lightly built, however, weighing up to 250 kg (551 lb).

FUN HOUSES

Igloos • Wigwams • Houseboats
Tree houses • Yurts

HAIRY HUMANS

Hairs on the body:
1,400,000–5,000,000

Head hairs on a blonde:
150,000

Head hairs on a brunette:
100,000

Head hairs on a redhead:
90,000

Hair grown in one year,
per person:
15 cm (6 in)

Number of hairs lost per day:
50–100

Longest hair ever:
5.15 m (16 ft 11 in)

Longest beard ever:
5.33 m (17 ft 4.9 in)

EXTREME IRONING

The weirdest places people have done their ironing are ...

... across a 30-m- (98-ft-) wide gorge at Wolfberg Cracks
in South Africa.

... parachuting off the side of a cliff in the Australian
Blue Mountains complete with an iron, board and laundry.

... on Mount Everest, at over 5,425 m (17,800 ft).

... while suspended underground at Alum Pot
in England's Yorkshire Dales.

... while running the London Marathon.

... underwater – especially when there's 50 people
doing it at once!

TEN FAMOUS VOLCANOES

Mount Etna, Sicily...Erupts almost constantly

Mount Fuji, Japan..Last erupted 1707

Mauna Loa, Hawaii...............................World's largest erupting volcano

Mount Vesuvius, Italy.............................Destroyed Pompeii in AD 79

Eyjafjallajökull, Iceland..................2010 eruption caused air traffic chaos

Mount Pinatubo, Philippines..........................Erupted in 1991 and 1994

Yellowstone, USA.....................................Recent signs suggest activity

Popocatépetl, Mexico...Last erupted 2005

Krakatoa, Indonesia..............................Enormous eruption in 1883

Mount Kilimanjaro, Tazmania......................Ice Age snow cap has almost completely melted away

WHICH DOORWAY?

You are trapped in a room. It is possible to get out but there's a snag. There are two doors through which you can leave, but while one leads to glorious freedom, the other will send you down into a bottomless pit from which there is no escape. And you don't know which door leads where. At each door stands a guard and you are allowed to ask one of them just one question to find out which door leads where. You know that one of the guards – you don't know which – invariably lies and the other always tells the truth. What should your question be?

('If you were the other guard, which door would you tell me leads to freedom?' You then take the other exit.)

A baby in Florida, USA, was recently named Truewilllaughinglifebuckyboomermanifestdestiny.

MEDIEVAL TORTURE INSTRUMENTS

THUMBSCREW
A vice-like instrument that crushed the victim's thumbs.

THE PRESS
A board under which the victim was secured, and on top of which increasingly heavy weights were piled.

THE BOOT
A box-like iron device into which the victim's foot was thrust. Wedges were then pushed in to crush the ankle.

THE PENDULUM
A swinging blade, suspended over the victim, which was gradually lowered until the victim either confessed, or was cut in two.

RED-HOT PINCERS
The torturer would pinch the victim in increasingly sensitive areas until the required information was received.

THE RACK
A frame on which the victim was tied by the wrists and ankles, and then stretched.

THE IRON CHAIR
A chair in which the victim was tied. A fire was then lit beneath to heat it to scorching temperatures.

THE IRON MAIDEN
A coffin-shaped box lined with spikes. The victim was made to get into it, and then it was slowly pushed shut.

FUNNY PLACE NAMES AROUND THE WORLD

Boom, Belgium

Burrumbuttock, New South Wales, Australia

Camel Hump, Wyoming, USA

Ding Dong, Texas, USA

Innaloo, Perth, Australia

Kau Shi Wai, Hong Kong
(said to mean 'village of dog poo' in Cantonese)

Louny, Czech Republic

Mumbles, Wales – to go with Mutters in Austria?

Nasty, Hertfordshire, England

No Place, County Durham, England

North Piddle, Worcestershire, England

Pratt's Bottom, London, England

Rottenegg, Austria

Titlis, Switzerland

Tubbercurry, County Sligo, Ireland

Turda, Cluj, Romania

Wagga Wagga, New South Wales, Australia

Where Reynolds Cut The Firewood, Pitcairn Island

Wong Way, Singapore

Zzyzx, California, USA

The richest woman in the world is Christy Walton, the daughter-in-law of Sam Walton, founder of the world's largest retailer, Wal-Mart. She is worth US $41.7 billion.

———— FOR YOUR ADDRESS BOOK ————

The President of the United States of America
The White House
1600 Pennsylvania Avenue NW
Washington, DC 20500
United States of America

Mr Harry Potter
The Cupboard Under the Stairs
4 Privet Drive
Little Whinging
Surrey
Great Britain

HM The Queen
Buckingham Palace
London SW1A 1AA
Great Britain

Coca-Cola Headquarters
1 Coca-Cola Plaza
Atlanta, GA 30313
United States of America

———— HOW LONG DO YOUR CELLS LIVE? ————

Stomach cells	Three days
Skin cells	Two to four weeks
Liver cells	Four to five months
Blood cells	Four to six months
Bone cells	Seven years
Brain cells	Can last a lifetime, but you lose 10,000–100,000 per day

Luckily, the body produces over a billion cells per hour.

THE 12 LABOURS OF HERCULES

Hercules was the son of a mortal woman and the ancient Greek god Zeus. Zeus's wife, the goddess Hera, was extremely jealous of Hercules and drove him to kill his own wife and children. As his penance, Hercules was sentenced to perform 12 seemingly impossible labours. He became Greece's greatest hero.

1. Kill the monster lion of Nemea and bring back its skin.

2. Kill the many-headed Hydra, a swamp-dwelling monster.

3. Capture alive the Hind of Ceryneia, a deer with golden horns and bronze hoofs that was sacred to the goddess Artemis.

4. Capture alive the enormous boar that lived on Mount Erymanthus.

5. Clean (in one day) the 30 years' worth of filth left by thousands of cattle in the Augean stables.

6. Drive away a huge flock of man-eating birds.

7. Bring back, alive, the mad bull that was terrorizing Crete.

8. Capture the man-eating mares of Diomedes, King of Thrace.

9. Retrieve the girdle of Hippolyta, Queen of the Amazons.

10. Steal the oxen that belonged to the three-headed (or, some say, three-bodied) monster Geryon.

11. Fetch Hera's golden apples that were closely guarded by nymphs, the Hesperides, with the help of a many-headed dragon.

12. Bring back alive, and without using weapons, Cerberus, the ferocious three-headed dog that guarded the underworld.

2B OR NOT 2B

The average pencil can draw a line about 56 km (35 miles) long, and can write up to 50,000 words. This is its story:

1560: A large deposit of graphite, a form of carbon, is discovered in Cumbria, England.

The locals use it to mark their sheep. It is thought to be a kind of lead and is named 'plumbago' after the Latin name for lead, *plumbum*.

People begin to wrap bits of sheepskin, string or fabric around their plumbago sticks.

The concept spreads to other countries, and in Italy they hit upon the idea of hollowing out sticks of juniper and sliding the plumbago in.

The writing tool becomes known as a pencil, from the Latin word for paintbrush, *peniculus*, which means 'little tail'.

Plumbago was renamed 'graphite', which comes from a Greek word meaning 'to write'.

1795: Nicholas Jacques Conté discovers that by mixing the graphite with clay he can vary the hardness, or darkness, of the pencil.

Today, pencils are graded 'H' for 'hardness' and
'B' for 'blackness':

9H • 8H • 7H • 6H • 5H • 4H • 3H • 2H (no. 4) • H (no. 3)
F (no. 2½) • HB (no. 2)
B (no. 1) • 2B • 3B • 4B • 5B • 6B • 7B • 8B • 9B

PIGPEN

Pigpen is a secret code that is very easy to use, but impossible to read if you don't know how it works. First of all you need to write out the whole alphabet in two grids, as shown below:

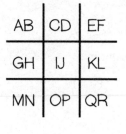

Each letter is represented by the part of the 'pigpen' that surrounds it. If it's the second letter in the box, then it has a dot in the middle. So, this:

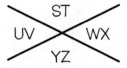

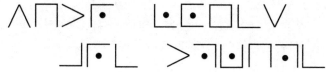

Translates as: Your flies are undone.

INSECT GRUB

Deep-fried scorpions • Three bee soup • Roasted grubs

Chocolate-covered locusts • Boiled silkworm larvae

Grasshoppers on toast • Tarantula sandwiches

Mealworm and chocolate chip cookies

> You share your birthday with at least nine million other people on earth.

'Jaws' is the most common name for a goldfish.

DAYS OF THE WEEK

All round the world the seven days of the week are named, directly or indirectly, after the Sun, Moon, and five planets visible to the naked eye: Mars, Mercury, Jupiter, Venus and Saturn.

Sunday	Day of the SUN
Monday	Day of the MOON
Tuesday	TYR'S day (Tyr is the Norse god of war, like the Roman god MARS)
Wednesday	WODEN'S day (Woden, or Odin, was identified with MERCURY)
Thursday	THOR'S day (Thor, the god of thunder, was identified with JUPITER, or Jove)
Friday	FREYA'S day (the goddess Freya is the Norse equivalent to the Roman VENUS)
Saturday	SATURN'S day

ABSENCE EXCUSE NOTES

Please excuse Jennifer for missing school yesterday. We forgot to get the Sunday paper off the porch, and when we found it on Monday, we thought it was Sunday.

William was absent from school on 8 May because it was a bank holiday in France and as we are part French we felt morally obliged to respect it here as well.

Flora was not in school yesterday because a badger nicked her alarm clock. (Tonight we might let her sleep in the shed instead of under the rose bush.)

Edward will no longer be attending school as he has been offered a job with the secret services. Please do not ask any further questions or we may have to kill you.

SUPER POWERS

Flight · Invisibility · X-ray vision · Elasticity
Super-human strength · Super speed · Telekinesis
Shape-shifting · Force fields · Healing · Cryokinesis (ice)
Pyrokinesis (fire) · Telepathy (mind reading)

If a statue of a person on a horse has both front legs in the air, the person died in a battle; if the horse has one front leg in the air, the person died as a result of injuries received in battle; if the horse has all four legs on the ground, the person died of natural causes.

A doctor in the USA is developing a way to grow vaccines in bananas and other fruits, so that instead of having an injection all you'll have to do is eat the fruit!

THEY SAY IT'S GOING TO RAIN IF ...

... frogs croak louder and longer than usual.

... dogs whine.

... roosters crow later in the day.

... birds fly lower to the ground and gather on tree branches and telephone wires.

... cows sit down in the fields to feed. Before a storm they run around the field with their tails high.

... bees and butterflies seem to disappear from the flower beds.

... fish jump out of the water to nip at low-flying insects.

OPPOSITES

Mend - Break	Catch - Throw
Over - Under	Cover - Expose
Decrease - Increase	Compliment - Insult
Transparent -Opaque	Find - Lose
Clean up - Mess up	Buy - Sell
Send - Receive	Fake - Genuine
Give - Take	Rough - Smooth

WHY YOU DON'T WANT TO MESS WITH CREEPY CRAWLIES

Insects outnumber human beings a million to one.

The total weight of insects in the world is at least three times the combined weight of all other living creatures.

The global populations of ants, fly beetles and springtails each outweigh the human race.

MORE 'FACTS' THAT ARE NOT TRUE

Lemmings commit mass suicide.

Finland once banned Donald Duck because he doesn't wear pants.

The Titanic was described by her owners as 'unsinkable'.

Coca-Cola was originally green.

The rhyme, Ring-a-Ring of Roses, is about the plague.

Ostriches bury their heads in the sand.

Tea contains more caffeine than coffee.

Eskimos have 400 words for snow.

CITY ANAGRAMS

Copenhagen	Hence, a pong!
Los Angeles	Sells an ego
Canberra	Barn race
Amsterdam	Edam, trams
Barcelona	Able acorn
New York	Worn key
Calcutta	Act a cult
Adelaide	A dead lie

IMPOSTERS

PRINCESS ANASTASIA a.k.a. Anna Anderson moved from Berlin to the USA when she married the American John Manahan. She claimed throughout her life that she was the sole survivor of the Russian royal family, murdered in 1918. She died in 1981, some ten years before DNA testing proved that she was not Anastasia.

TUESDAY LOBSANG RAMPA was famous for his books about spirituality and his childhood in Tibet, and became a lama (a Buddhist monk). When he was found to actually be an Englishman called Cyril Hoskins, he insisted that his body had been taken over by the lama one Tuesday, and went on writing his books. He died in 1981.

THE TICHBORNE CLAIMANT travelled from Australia to England under a fake name in 1866 and duped Lady Tichborne into believing he was her long-lost son and heir to the baronetcy.

GEORGE PSALMANAZAR fooled people all over 18th-century Europe into believing he was a cannibal prince from an exotic eastern land, publishing books about his native country and even teaching at Oxford University, England.

PRINCESS CARABOO enjoyed many weeks of celebrity in 1817 as a princess from 'Javasu' who'd been kidnapped by pirates and had escaped. Her fun was spoiled when she was recognized as Mary Baker, a servant girl.

WEALTHIEST FICTIONAL CHARACTERS

1. Scrooge McDuck
2. Smaug, *The Hobbit*
3. Carlisle Cullen, *Twilight*
4. Tony Stark, *Iron Man*
5. Charles Kane, *Citizen Kane*
6. Bruce Wayne, *Batman*
7. Richie Rich, *Richie Rich*
8. Christian Grey, *50 Shades of Grey*
9. Tywin Lannister, *Game of Thrones*
10. Mr Burns, *The Simpsons*

THE CONTINENTS

Africa • North America • South America
Antarctica • Asia • Australasia • Europe

The first letter of each continent's
name is the same as its last.

Asia has the largest land area, largest population
and the highest mountains.

Australasia is the smallest continent.

Europe has the highest ratio of coastline to total area.

During your lifetime, you will eat about 60,000 pounds
of food – the weight of about six elephants!

CARD TRICK

Take all 13 cards from one suit, e.g. hearts,
and secretly arrange them in this order:

3, 8, 7, ace, king, 6, 4, 2, queen, knave, 10, 9, 5

Put the rest of the cards to one side.

Hold the 13 cards in a pile face down with the 3 at the top
and say to your audience, 'A-C-E spells ace.' As you say
each letter, take the card from the top of the pack and place
it at the bottom. When you say 'ace' turn the top card over
and show them that it is the ace.

Do the same again saying, 'T-W-O spells two' and showing
that the top card this time is the 2. Repeat with the other
cards all the way up to K-I-N-G and amaze your friends
as you spell out the correct card every time!

Make sure you spell out K-N-A-V-E instead of J-A-C-K
or the trick won't work.

SAY WHAT YOU SEE

BAD wolf

Big bad wolf

Sunny side up

~~MY HEART~~

Cross my heart

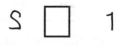

Back to square one

YOURANTSPANTS

Ants in your pants

Head over heels in love

SHUT

SIT

Shut up and sit down

Wish upon a star

HOTTEST, COLDEST, DRIEST, WETTEST

HIGHEST TEMPERATURE RECORDED
On 10 July 1913 the temperature in Greenland Ranch, Death Valley, California, USA, reached a scorching 56.7°C (134°F).

LONGEST HOT SPELL
For 162 consecutive days (30 October–7 April 1924) in Marble Bar, Western Australia, the temperature never dropped below 37.8°C (100°F).

LOWEST TEMPERATURE RECORDED
On 21 July 1983 the temperature in Vostok, Antarctica, plummeted to -89.2°C (-128.6°F).

LOWEST AVERAGE ANNUAL TEMPERATURE
At Plateau Station in Antarctica the average temperature is -56.7°C (-70°F).

DRIEST REGION
In some parts of Antarctica it hasn't rained at all for over two million years.

WETTEST PLACE
In Mawsynram, Meghalaya, India, there is approximately 11,873 mm (467 in) of rain per year.

LARGEST HAILSTONE
A ginormous hailstone measuring 20.3 cm (8 in) in diameter and 47.3 cm (18.63 in) in circumference, landed in South Dakota, USA on 23 July 2010.

Your brain uses 13 per cent less energy when you sit watching television than when you do nothing at all.

A swarm of locusts covering an area of 5,180 square kilometres (2,000 square miles) crossed the Red Sea in 1889. It was estimated to weigh 500,000 tons and contain 250 thousand million locusts.

THE OLYMPIC GAMES

776 BC   First Olympic Games held at Olympia, Greece.
It was a one-day event consisting of a 200-metre race.

472 BC   The games are increased to five days, to allow for
new activities such as boxing and wrestling.

1896   The modern Olympics, a revival of the Olympian
Games, are held in Athens, largely thanks to the
French sportsman Baron Pierre de Coubertin. The
event continues to be held every four years.

1924   The Winter Olympics, held in the same year as the
Summer Olympics, are added to the Olympic calendar.

1994   The International Olympic Committee decides to
hold the Winter and Summer Olympics on alternate
even years.

2012   London hosts the Summer Olympics for a record third
time. It first hosted the games in 1908, then again in 1948.

The Olympic motto is 'Citius, Altius, Fortius' – 'Swifter, Higher,
Stronger'. The Olympic symbol is a white background with five
interlocking circles coloured blue, yellow, black, green and red,
representing the five continents. At least one of those colours
appears in the national flag of every country.

WHAT'S BLACK AND WHITE AND RED ALL OVER?

A newspaper • A sunburnt nun • An embarrassed zebra

A penguin with chicken pox • A dalmatian holding its breath

A vampire who's spilled his dinner down himself

A skunk in a blender

FAMOUS GHOSTS

THE WHISTLESTOP GHOST

A bearded man in a grey coat who has haunted a train-station café in Waitakere, New Zealand since the 1920s. The mysterious figure is said to be a man who was hit by a passing train.

TRIANON PALACE

On the 10 August 1901, two English women seemed to slip back in time while visiting the palace at Versailles in France. They felt a strange sense of gloom and loneliness, and then encountered a series of figures in 18th-century dress. They later discovered that the grounds were said to be haunted by Marie Antoinette and her court, and that a bridge they crossed had been destroyed many years earlier.

LA LLORONA

The ghost of a Mexican woman who fell in love with a nobleman and killed her children so that she could be with him (he didn't much fancy having a load of kids to look after). She then became so grief-stricken that she killed herself. To this day she roams the land, weeping and looking for her lost children.

THE ROSENHEIM POLTERGEIST

From 1967 to 1969 a solicitor's office in Germany was affected by strange phenomena witnessed by over 40 people. Lights flickered, bulbs fell out of their sockets, telephone calls were cut off, pictures rotated on the walls, and filing cabinets moved by themselves.

MIXING COLOUR

PAINT

red + yellow = orange

yellow + blue = green

blue + red = purple

red + yellow + blue = brown

LIGHT

red + green = yellow

green + blue = cyan

blue + red = magenta

red + green + blue = white

THE FATE OF THE CHILDREN IN
CHARLIE AND THE CHOCOLATE FACTORY

AUGUSTUS GLOOP - In his greed to devour chocolate, falls in the chocolate river and is sucked up into a pipe to be taken to the strawberry fudge room.

VIOLET BEAUREGARDE - Disregards Mr Wonka's warning and eats an experimental meal in chewing-gum form; when she gets to the pudding, blueberry pie, she turns into a giant blueberry and is taken away to have the juice squeezed out of her.

VERUCA SALT - Tries to take a trained nut-testing squirrel, but the squirrels test her and she is thrown down the bad-nut chute into a disgusting rubbish dump in the basement.

MIKE TEAVEE - Disobeys Mr Wonka and tries to send himself across the room via television. He miniaturizes himself in the process.

CHARLIE BUCKET - Because he isn't greedy or naughty or vain or addicted to television, is the only remaining child, and Mr Wonka hands the factory over to him.

HOW TO CHEAT

Speak all the answers on to a tape machine and tell the teacher that you find it relaxing to listen to music through earphones.

Write the answers on your sleeve.

Paste the cover of your textbook over the study guide and take that in instead.

Make friends with a kid from another school who takes the exam the day before.

Phone a friend.

Get someone to take the exam for you.

Faint.

Shout 'Fire!' and sneak a peak at the other papers on your way out.

WHAT TEACHERS REALLY MEAN

'Good morning.'
Please, don't throw anything.

'What page are we on?'
I've completely forgotten what I've been teaching you.

'We're going to work in groups today, then you can present your ideas to the class.'
I'm too tired to teach – you lot can do the work.

WHY IS THE SKY BLUE?

Light is made up of different colours that we can see separately when we look at a rainbow. Some of these colours travel through air and dust quite easily, but blue light gets bounced around by molecules of air. So when you look up at the sky, you are really seeing miles and miles of blue light in the air. The sea appears to be blue because it reflects the sky.

EVERYDAY INVENTIONS

Wooden coat-hangers............Thomas Jefferson, c.1790

Tea bags....................................Thomas Sullivan, 1908

Frozen food................................Clarence Birdseye, 1925

Ballpoint pens...László Biró, 1938

Velcro...Georges de Mestral, 1948

Computer games.................................A.S. Douglas, 1952

Digital wristwatch...............................Sir Clive Sinclair, 1976

CDs..Toshi Tada Doi, 1979

World Wide Web..............................Tim Berners-Lee, 1989

Facebook.......................................Mark Zuckerberg, 2004

COUNTRIES WITH THE MOST TRACTORS PER HECTARE OF FARMLAND

Iceland

Slovenia

Japan

Switzerland

Austria

ANNOYING THINGS TEACHERS ALWAYS SAY

'I don't care who started it.'

'Something's obviously very funny, so why don't you share it with the rest of us?'

'This is for your benefit, so please wake up.'

'Honestly, it's like talking to a brick wall sometimes.'

'I'd expect that kind of behaviour from them, but really, I'm surprised at you.'

'If you're so clever, why don't you come up here and take the lesson?'

'Would you do that at home?'

'Come on. We're waiting.'

MUSIC GENRES

Classical

Jazz

Folk

R & B/Soul

Rock

Country

Electronic

Dance

Reggae

Pop

Easy Listening

World

Latin

Opera

Blues

Rap

NAMES OF THE MONTHS

The word 'month' comes from 'moon', because months were once measured from full moon to full moon (about 29 days). In Roman times, there used to be just ten months in the year, and the first was March:

March	Named after Mars, the Roman god of war
April	From the Latin 'aperire' meaning 'to open'
May	Named after Maia, goddess of spring
June	Named after Juno, queen of Roman gods
Quintilis	Latin for 'fifth'
Sextilis	Latin for 'sixth'
September	From the Latin for 'seventh'
October	From the Latin for 'eighth'
November	From the Latin for 'ninth'
December	From the Latin for 'tenth'

Then, in the 7th century BC, two months were added at the beginning of the year:

January	Named after the Roman god of gateways
February	From the religious purification ritual 'februum' that took place that month. The festival was named after Februus, the Etruscan god of the dead and of purification.

This is why our ninth month is called the seventh (September), and so on.

In 44 BC, Julius Caesar decided a month should be named after him:
July	Used to be Quintilis, re-named after Julius Caesar

Augustus Caesar thought this was a great idea:
August	Used to be 'Sextilis', re-named after Augustus Caesar

SEVEN SPELLS FROM HARRY POTTER

Alohamora – To open a locked door.

Colloportus – To seal a door (with a squelch).

Expecto Patronum – To conjure up a Patronus
(used to drive away Dementors etc.).

Impedimenta – To stop or slow something down.

Incendio – To start a fire.

Petrificus Totalus – To turn someone 'to stone'.

Tarantallegra – To cause someone to dance madly.

HOW TO FAKE A SMILE

Because smiling releases endorphins, even faking a smile can improve a person's mood. There are different types of smiles – 'felt' smiles, which are explosions of joy and happiness, and 'social' smiles (said to number 18 different kinds – smiles of greeting, thanks, reassurance etc.). People can differentiate between felt and social smiles; in felt smiles the muscles that raise the cheekbones also contract, making the eyes crease up, and the eyebrows dip slightly. Smiling is infectious – smile at someone and the likelihood is that they'll smile back.

THE CHAIR OF TRUTH

To play this trick on a friend, place a sponge soaked with water on a chair that has a slatted seat (one that will allow water to drain through). Cover the sponge up with a towel and drape towels and cushions all over the chair to disguise what you have done. Finally, place an empty tin upside down underneath the chair.

Ask your friend to stand next to the Chair of Truth while you ask him or her some questions. After each answer, look at the chair and say 'the Chair of Truth agrees that you have answered honestly.'

Now ask your friend the question: 'What is the last thing you do each night before you go to bed?' They will probably answer that they clean their teeth, or read a book, or have a drink of water. Look at the chair and say 'The Chair of Truth says that you are lying. You must sit on the chair so that I can know the truth.'

When your friend sits on the chair the water will drain from the sponge, through the slats and make a loud dripping noise on the tin beneath.

'The Chair of Truth says that the last thing you do before you go to sleep at night is go to the toilet.'

RABBIT OR DUCK?

Each foot has over 250,000 sweat glands and produces approximately half a pint of sweat in just a day one! The horrible smell is caused not by the sweat but by bacteria that eat the sweat and excrete strong-smelling waste. In the damp cosy darkness of our socks and shoes, these microbes feast away merrily and the more sweat the smellier. Armpits are another nice, warm, cosy, sweaty place for bacteria to feast.

A ROMAN BANQUET SET MENU

DRINK
Spiced wine
Water
(Please note that slaves will frequently refill your cup)

STARTER
Gustatio, consisting of sea urchins with
spices, oil and egg sauce
Jellyfish and eggs
Milk-fed snails fried in oil

MAIN COURSE
Deer roasted with onion sauce
Dates, raisins and honey
Boiled flamingo in a spicy sauce
Roast boar stuffed with small birds
Sausages and vegetables
Baked dormice stuffed with pork and pine kernels
Roast parrot with dates
Jugs of *garum* and *liquamen* (sauces made from
fermented fish)

DESSERT
Dates with almonds and honey
Roses baked in pastry
Dates stuffed with nuts and pine kernels, fried in honey

GRAND PRIX: TEN FORMULA 1 CHAMPIONS

1. Alain Prost (McLaren-TAG/Porsche) 1985, 1986; (McLaren-Honda) 1989; (Williams-Renault) 1993
2. Michael Schumacher (Benetton-Ford) 1994; (Benetton-Renault) 1995; (Ferrari) 2000, 2001, 2002, 2003, 2004
3. Damon Hill (Williams-Renault) 1996
4. Jacques Villeneuve (Williams-Renault) 1997
5. Mika Hakkinen (McLaren-Mercedes) 1998, 1999
6. Fernando Alonso (Renault) 2005, 2006
7. Kimi Räikkönen (Ferrari) 2007
8. Lewis Hamilton (McLaren-Mercedes) 2008; (Mercedes) 2014
9. Jenson Button (Brawn-Mercedes) 2009
10. Sebastian Vettel (Red Bull-Renault) 2010, 2011, 2012, 2013

> In a survey 54 per cent of people said they fold toilet paper neatly to wipe; 35 per cent bunch it up into a ball. What the remaining 11 per cent do was not recorded.

THE FIVE DEADLIEST PLACES ON EARTH

TAKLAMAKAN DESERT
Located in north-west China, further from the ocean than any other place on earth, it receives almost no rain. It is boiling hot in summer, prone to dust storms and is used as a nuclear weapons testing ground.

ANNAPURNA MOUNTAIN
With more than five avalanches a day, this mountain in Nepal has the highest death toll of any climbing peak in the world.

SHARK ALLEY
Just off the coast of Cape Town in South Africa, this channel between two islands is infested with sharks who sometimes mistake humans for their usual diet of seals.

LA PAZ TO COROICO ROAD
The 64-km- (39.77-mile-) long trail in the mountains of Bolivia is also known as the 'Death Road'. It is very narrow, very steep, and runs along the edge of a deep valley. There is a fatal accident there about once a fortnight.

AMBOPATA RESERVE
One of the most remote parts of the Amazon jungle, it is home to the wandering spider (the most deadly spider in the world), stinging ants, killer caterpillars, deadly vipers, skin-crawling bicho worms, piranha fish and many other death-inducing creatures.

LANGUAGES OF WIDER COMMUNICATION

Some people believe that an international language might solve world problems that are caused by misunderstandings of communication. The most successful international languages are:

ENGLISH: Widely spoken, and is the international language used by aeroplane pilots.

ESPERANTO: An invented language with straightforward grammar and simple pronunciation.

LOGLAN: A laboratory-created language designed to be easy enough for anyone from any culture to learn.

ART MOVEMENTS

Classical	Fauvism
Renaissance	Modernism
Mannerism	Expressionism
Baroque	Cubism
Rococo	Dadaism
Romanticism	Surrealism
Pre-Raphaelite	Abstraction
Symbolism	Pop Art
Realism	Op Art
Impressionism	Postmodernism

HOMEMADE INVISIBLE INK

1. Mix one spoon of baking powder with one to two spoons of cold water.
2. Dip a toothpick or cotton bud in the mixture and use it to write your message on a piece of white paper.
3. Wait for the ink to dry.
4. Hold the paper up to a light bulb and the message will appear.
5. Alternatively, paint the paper with purple grape juice to reveal the secret message.

MOONS OF JUPITER

Metis	Io	Leda	Ananke
Adrastea	Europa	Himalia	Carme
Amalthea	Ganymede	Lysithea	Pasiphaë
Thebe	Callisto	Elara	Sinope

UNIDENTIFIED FLYING OBJECTS

Theories as to what UFOs could be include:

Aircraft or airships • Weather balloons • Kites • Parachutes

Insect swarms • Clouds so high they reflect the sun at night

The Northern Lights • Meteor showers or comets

Ball lightning • Secret military operations

SOME INTERESTING SIGHTINGS

Norfolk, UK, 26-28 December 1980: men from an RAF airbase in the area saw an airborne object and strange bright lights. The next day investigators found broken branches and three small circular depressions in the soil.

Minsk, USSR (now Russia), 7 September 1984: the pilots of a Soviet Aeroflot airliner reported seeing a strange, brightly glowing form that followed their path for several minutes, changing shape repeatedly. A second flight crew travelling in the opposite direction also reported seeing a glowing object. A Soviet missile was being launched at the time – but in order to protect military secrets, Soviet officials denied the missile's existence.

Brussels, Belgium, 30 March 1990: two F-16 fighter pilots were sent to intercept an unexplained object detected by radar. It was night. They locked their radar on the object, but it sped away; they chased it for 75 minutes, then lost it.

TANGRAMS

Tangrams were first created in ancient China. A square is divided into seven pieces (as shown). The aim is then to combine the seven shapes to create images or symbols, typically of weird and wonderful people, animals or objects.

——— THE LONGEST PLACE NAMES IN THE WORLD ———

Krung Thep Mahanakhon Amon Rattanakosin Mahinthara
Ayuthaya Mahadilok Phop Noppharat Ratchathani
Burirom Udomratchaniwet Mahasathan Amon Piman
Awatan Sathit Sakkathattiya Witsanukam Prasit

At 21 words/168 letters long, this ceremonial name for Thailand's capital city Krung Thep or, as we know it, Bangkok, is the longest place name in the world. It means:

'The city of angels, the great city, the eternal jewel city, the impregnable city of God Indra, the grand capital of the world endowed with nine precious gems, the happy city, abounding in an enormous Royal Palace that resembles the heavenly abode where reigns the reincarnated god, a city given by Indra and built by Vishnukarn.'

The longest single-word place name belongs to a town in
New Zealand called

Tetaumatawhakatangihangakoauaotamateaurehaeaturipukapihimaungahoronukupokaiwhenuaakitanarahu

It is 92 letters long and means:

'The brow of the hill [or place], where Tamatea,
the man with the big knees, who slid [down], climbed [up]
and swallowed mountains, [to travel the land], [and is] known as
the Land Eater, played [on] his [nose] flute to his loved one.'

——— GROUND-TO-AIR CODE ———

MESSAGE	CODE SYMBOL
We need help	V
We need a doctor	X
Yes	Y
No	N
It should be safe to land here	△
We've gone this way	→

FIVE FAMOUS HOAXES

THE CARDIFF GIANT
(New York, USA, 1869)
Workmen found the fossilized remains of a huge man buried in the grounds of a farm. Eventually, two men admitted that they had made the giant bones out of a calcium-based substance called gypsum.

THE COTTINGLEY FAIRIES
(Yorkshire, England, 1917)
Elsie Wright (15) and her cousin Frances Griffiths (10) fooled the world with their photographs of fairies. It was not until 1983 that they explained they had cut the fairies out of a book!

PILTDOWN MAN
(Sussex, England, 1912)
Scientists were presented with the fossil remains of what was claimed to be the 'missing link' between man and ape. It was not until 1953 that modern testing methods showed it to be a very clever patchwork of human skull, orangutan jawbone and elephant and hippo teeth. The hoaxer has never been identified.

HITLER'S DIARIES
(Germany, 1983)
A reputable German journal announced its scoop – 62 volumes of Adolf Hitler's diaries – for which they had paid an enormous sum. In their excitement, they had missed a lot of historical inaccuracies and failed to carry out proper tests – it soon became apparent that the diaries were a hoax carried out by a dealer in documents.

THE AMITYVILLE HORROR
(New York, USA, 1974)
George and Katy Lutz moved into a house in which a man had shot his parents and four siblings dead. A month later they moved out again, and published the story of their experiences in the house – complete with tales of swarms of flies, demonic cats, ghostly apparitions, green slime ... the lot. The couple made a great deal of money out of it, then admitted in 1979 that they had concocted the whole story.

Time flies like an arrow, fruit flies like bananas.

FIVE WAYS TO DE-SMELL YOUR TRAINERS

1. A couple of drops of peppermint oil.
2. Fill a sock with cat litter (preferably unused)
   and leave in the trainer overnight.
3. Put a fabric-softener sheet in the bottom of the trainer.
4. Dust the inside of the trainer with baby powder.
5. Leave a few unused tea bags in the shoe for two days.

CELEBRITY DRAGONS

Draco..................................Teams up with the dragonslayer in *Dragonheart*

Dragon..Falls in love with Donkey in *Shrek*

Horntail Dragon..........Appears in *Harry Potter and the Goblet of Fire*

Toothless..From *How to Train Your Dragon*

Smaug...In *The Hobbit* by J.R.R. Tolkien

Norbert........................Hagrid's baby dragon in *Harry Potter and the
Philosopher's Stone*

WHAT ANIMALS SAY

SHEEP
'baa' (English)
'bee hee' (Croatian)
'maeh' (Danish)
'bee-bee' (Slovenian)

PIGS
'gron-gron' (French)
'ha-roo' (Russian)
'oot-oot' (Thai)
'moo-moo' (Japanese)

DOGS
'ouaf-ouaf' (French)
'brippi brippi' (Italian)
'gong gong' (Indonesian)
'bahk-bahk' (Thai)
'wan-wan' (Japanese)
'gahf-gahft' (Russian)
'wang wang' (Chinese)

COWS
'oo-ah' (Thai)
'meuh' (French)
'moo' (English)

COCKERELS
'cock-a-doodle-doo' (English)
'kickerikie' (German)
'cocorico' (French)

CATS
'neow' (Japanese)
'miaou' (French)
'miaow' (English)
'mao' (Thai)

BEES
'buzz-buzz' (English)
'bhon-bhon' (Bengali)
'wing-wing' (Korean)

WHAT BLUE MEANS

Life • Spirituality • Loyalty • Fidelity • Peace • Tranquillity
Sadness • Depression • Mourning • Dreaminess
Reliability • Authority

RAINBOWS – THE TRUTH AND THE LIES

TRUTH: A RAINBOW IS BENT LIGHT

Sunlight passes through drops of rainwater, which act like little prisms and bend the light and then reflect it back from the surface of the drops. The amount of bending, known as refraction, differs for light of different colours - red light bends the least and violet light bends the most.

LIE: THERE IS GOLD AT THE END OF THE RAINBOW

Rainbows are in fact circular, and therefore don't have 'ends'.

TRUTH: RICHARD OF YORK GAVE BATTLE IN VAIN

This is a 'mnemonic' to help you remember the colours of the rainbow: Red, Orange, Yellow, Green, Blue, Indigo, Violet.

LIE: THERE ARE SEVEN COLOURS IN THE RAINBOW

There are really only six - indigo is just the blue fading into the violet, but Sir Isaac Newton, who investigated light and colour, was a superstitious man, and believed seven to be a lucky number.

TRUTH: A HIGH SUN CAUSES A LOW RAINBOW

When the sun is more than 42 degrees above the horizon, no rainbow is visible.

NAME THAT BAND

COLDPLAY - They were originally called Starfish. Friends of theirs were in a band called Coldplay, but did not carry on and let them have the name. The original band got the name from a collection of poems by Philip Horky.

OASIS - They changed their name from Rain after getting the idea from a poster for a gig by the Inspiral Carpets at the Oasis Leisure Centre in Swindon.

DAFT PUNK - Got their name from a review of their previous band Darlin'. The review called them 'a bunch of daft punk'.

MAROON 5 - Refuse to tell anyone the origins of the band's name because it's such a horrendous story.

BIRTHSTONES

January..Garnet

February...Amethyst

March...Bloodstone

April..Diamond

May...Emerald

June...Pearl

July...Ruby

August...Sardonyx

September..Sapphire

October..Opal

November...Topaz

December...Turquoise

Spun sugar is called candy floss in the UK, *barbe à papa* in France, *zuckerwatte* in Germany, fairy floss in Australia and cotton candy in the United States.

HOW TO WHISTLE ON GRASS

1. To find a suitable blade of grass, look for one that is long and at least a quarter of an inch wide.

2. Trap the blade of grass between the outer edges of your thumbs, when they are pressed together with the nails facing towards you.

3. You should be able to see the blade of glass in the gap just below the joints of your thumbs.

4. Press your lips to the gap and blow.

5. If you don't produce a whistle at first, keep adjusting the position of your lips and the grass until you get it right.

THINGS THAT THERE SHOULD BE WORDS FOR THAT THERE AREN'T

The strangely pleasant feeling of desperately needing the toilet.

The feeling of disappointment you get when you receive the same present twice.

An itch that you can only get rid of by scratching another part of your body.

The shock of hearing your own name spoken during a daydream in class.

The extra-delicious taste that food has when you can only have one mouthful.

The far-away feeling you get in your head when you read something out loud in front of lots of people.

The love you feel for someone (usually a brother or sister) that can only be expressed by annoying them.

The shame of being told off by a friend's parent.

Outer space begins 100 km (62 miles) above the Earth's surface. The line where outer space begins is called the Kármán line.

A BILLION AGO

A billion seconds ago, your parents were children.

A billion minutes ago, the Roman Empire was booming.

A billion hours ago, Neanderthals lived in Europe and Asia.

A billion months ago, dinosaurs ruled the Earth.

A billion years ago, primitive life evolved.

THE DIFFERENCE BETWEEN TANGERINES, SATSUMAS, CLEMENTINES AND ORANGES

ORANGE

Thought to be a cross between a pomelo (a pale-green fruit bigger than a grapefruit) and a tangerine. (A grapefruit is a cross between a pomelo and an orange.)

MANDARIN ORANGE

Resembles an orange, but is shaped like a flattened sphere. It comes in several varieties including the tangerine, satsuma and clementine.

SATSUMA

Sweet, seedless and smaller than an orange. The skin can be peeled easily. First exported from Satsuma Province in Japan, where satsumas are called mikan.

TANGOR

A cross between a mandarin and an orange. Thin, easy-to-peel rind and pale-orange pulp that tastes spicy and tart.

CLEMENTINE

Smooth, glossy, vibrant orange skin that is thin and easy to peel. They separate easily into eight to 12 juicy, sweet-tasting segments.

TANGERINE

Has dimpled skin that peels off easily. Smaller than an orange, but heavy for its size. The name comes from Tangier, a port in Morocco from which the first tangerines were shipped to Europe.

THE LAYERS OF EARTH'S ATMOSPHERE

Troposphere...0–14.5 km (0–9 miles) above Earth

Stratosphere...14.5–50 km (9–31 miles) above Earth

Mesosphere...50–85 km (31–53 miles) above Earth

Thermosphere...85–600 km (53–372 miles) above Earth

Exosphere...600 km+ (372 miles+) above Earth

SMELLY CHEESES

Vieux Boulogne

Pont l'Évêque

Munster

Camembert

Gammelost

Limburger

Brie de Meaux

Roquefort

Reblochon

Livarot

Banon

Gorgonzola

Époisses de Bourgogne

Stinking Bishop

REAL SONIC WEAPONS

Sonic weapons are weapons that use sound
waves to deter or injure the enemy.

INFRASONIC SIREN
Modern cruise ships
have experimented with
infrasonic sirens to repel
the enemy at sea. The low-
frequency sound can make
concrete walls crumble
and humans violently ill.

ANTI-FROGMAN WEAPON
A ship can sound its ordinary
navigation sonar to deter
enemy scuba divers. The
sound waves make divers
disorientated and they either
panic and drown, or are
forced to the surface.

SONIC BULLETS
These high-power
beams of ultrasound can
measure up to 145 decibels
loud. The sound waves stop
people in their tracks.

INFRASONIC GUN
In the 1950s the first
infrasonic gun was
immediately classified as
'almost lethal' when it made
the internal organs of the test
subjects bleed. The gun made
the laboratory shake violently,
even on low power.

THINGS NOT TO TREAD ON WHEN PADDLING IN THE SEA

Portuguese man-of-war......................................Jellyfish with stinging tentacles

Stinging seaweed...........................Venomous animal disguised as a plant

Fire coral.............................Looks like coral but has stinging tentacles

Stonefish................................Looks like a stone but has poisonous spines

Sea urchin................Has poisonous spines that break off in your foot

Stingray................................Fish with a razor-sharp spine and stinging tail that lies in the sand

Blue-ringed octopus..........................The size of a tennis ball, with poison powerful enough to kill a human in minutes

INEXPENSIVE COLLECTIBLES

Chewing-gum packets • Aeroplane sick bags
Crisp packets • Rubber ducks • Matchboxes
Train tickets • Four-leaf clovers • Fruit stickers
Human teeth • Buttons • Ballpoint pens
Fridge magnets • Fizzy-drink cans

PHASES OF THE MOON

On average, the Moon takes 29.5 days to complete one orbit around the Earth. This is known as a lunar month. During this time, the Moon goes through a complete cycle from new Moon to full Moon and back again. The phases are:

1.
Dark Moon or
New Moon

2.
Waxing-crescent
Moon

3.
First-quarter
Moon

4.
Waxing-gibbous
Moon

5.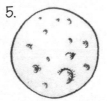
Full Moon

6.
Waning-gibbous
Moon

7.
Last-quarter
Moon

8.
Waning-crescent
Moon

9.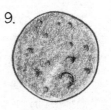
Dark Moon or
New Moon

In the southern hemisphere, the above is reversed so that a waxing-crescent Moon is seen as the left side of the Moon, and a waning-crescent Moon is seen as the right side of the Moon.

> Paraguay is the only country in the world whose national flag has two different sides.

POISONOUS PLANTS

Deadly nightshade • Hemlock

Holly • Death cap mushroom

Mistletoe • Iris • Yew

HOW TO KEEP A DIARY

1. Try to write in your diary regularly, even if it is not every day.

2. Find a quiet place where you won't be disturbed while writing.

3. Write the date, time and place at the beginning of each entry.

4. Keep mementos such as photos, cinema tickets and party invitations in your diary.

5. Be as honest as you can about your thoughts and feelings.

6. Find a good hiding place for your diary. You could disguise it by covering it with a dust jacket belonging to a boring book and putting it on your bookshelf.

7. If you're still worried about someone finding it, write a few dull entries in a decoy diary and leave it somewhere obvious.

FAST FLIERS

Peregrine falcon	286 kph (240 mph)
Spine-tailed swift	171 kph (106 mph)
Frigate bird	153 kph (95 mph)
Spur-winged goose	142 kph (88 mph)
Red-breasted merganser	129 kph (80 mph)

REAL-LIFE SUPERHEROES

STRETCHY MAN

British man Gary Turner can stretch his skin to a length of 15.8 cm (6.2 in). By pulling the skin of his neck up and the skin of his forehead down, he can completely cover his whole face. On 27 November 2004, he clipped 159 wooden clothes pegs to his face, earning himself a world record.

MR EAT EVERYTHING

In 1959, Michel Lotito of France developed a taste for metal and glass. So far he has eaten 18 bicycles, 15 supermarket trolleys, seven TVs, two beds, one pair of skis and one Cessna light aircraft.

THE HUMAN LIGHTNING CONDUCTOR

Roy C. Sullivan of the USA has been struck by lightning no fewer than seven times. He has survived each strike, but suffered the following injuries:

1942, lost a big toenail

1969, lost both eyebrows

1970, left shoulder burned

1972, hair caught fire

1973, legs burned, hair singed

1976, ankle hurt

1977, stomach and chest burned

COUNTRIES WHOSE NAMES BEGIN AND END WITH THE SAME LETTER

Albania	Australia
Algeria	Austria
Andorra	Czech Republic
Angola	St. Kitts and Nevis
Antigua and Barbuda	St. Vincent and the Grenadines
Argentina	Seychelles
Armenia	Solomon Islands

THE THREE-CARD-MONTE SCAM

1. The scammer shows three playing cards to the audience. One of the cards is a queen.

2. The three cards are placed face-down on a table.

3. The scammer moves the cards around, changing their positions, then invites the audience to place bets on which one is the queen.

4. If the audience are sceptical and hang back, an accomplice places a bet and wins.

5. Encouraged by this, the audience start placing bets.

6. The scammer secretly swaps the queen for a different card to ensure that the members of the audience always lose.

7. To keep the bets coming in, every so often the scammer secretly reintroduces the queen and lets someone win. If he is a successful con artist, no one will even realize they are being conned.

BIRD CALLS

Tawny owl...'Hoo hoo-hooo hoo-o-o'

Peregrine falcon.................'Haak-haak-haak kee-keeee-eeee wheee-ip'

Wren...'Chit chiti tzerr'

Blue tit...'Tsee-tsee-tsee-tsisisisisisi'

Nuthatch..'Pew pew pew chwee chwee'

Bittern...'Boom ker-whoomp'

Middle-spotted woodpecker...................'Kvek-kvek-kvek kuk-uk kuk-uk'

Brent goose...'Kurr-onk kurr-onk kurr-onk'

Laughing gull.................................'hah-hah-hah hoo-hoo hah-hah-hah'

Wood pigeon................'Coo-ooo-coo-cu-ooo coo-coo-cu-coo'

Egyptian vulture...'Silent'

TEN RULES OF DUELLING

1. You may use a duel to restore honour if someone has offended you.

2. Challenges are never delivered at night.

3. The duel must take place within a month of the challenge being delivered.

4. The challenged has the right to choose the weapon and the location of the duel.

5. Each combatant nominates a 'second' of equal rank in society. The second acts as a go-between - first attempting reconciliation between the parties, and then, if this fails, fixing the time and terms of the duel.

6. The duellists start at an agreed distance from each other, armed with swords or pistols.

7. Seconds must reattempt reconciliation after the specified time or number of shots or blows.

8. In the case of pistols, a misfire is counted as a shot.

9. If seconds disagree on anything, they may themselves duel. They should position themselves at right-angles to the challengers to form a cross.

10. Any wound that causes the hand to shake ends the duel.

FUN DUELLING WEAPONS

Bananas
Water pistols
Flour bombs
Snowballs
Light sabres
Custard pies
Paper aeroplanes
Back-to-front speaking

BUBBLEGUM

The first bubblegum was developed in 1906.
It was named 'Blibber-Blubber'.

In 1928, the bubblegum recipe was improved by an
American called Walter Diemer, resulting in the first widely sold
bubblegum, 'Dubble Bubble'. Diemer coloured his creation
pink because it was the only food colouring he had.

Today over 100,000 tons of bubblegum are chewed every year.

HOW TO BLOW A BUBBLEGUM BUBBLE

1. Put a big piece of bubblegum in your mouth.

2. Chew it until it's thin and stretchy.

3. Use your tongue to flatten the gum across the backs of your top and bottom front teeth.

4. Push the middle of the gum out between your teeth while forming a seal all the way around the gum with your lips.

5. Blow into the stretched gum.

TIPS FOR REMOVING GUM FROM HAIR AND CLOTHING

1. Rub the gum with an ice cube. This will harden the gum, making it easier to pick and scratch off.

2. Squeeze lemon juice on the gum. This will help reduce its stickiness.

3. Put a few drops of cooking oil or peanut butter on a toothbrush and scrub the gum.

> The advertising slogan 'Pepsi gives you life'
> was mistranslated in Chinese to 'Pepsi brings
> your ancestors back from the grave.'

PLACES TO HIDE A SECRET MESSAGE

Under a loose floorboard • In the notch of a tree

Under your mattress • On the ledge inside a chimney

Behind a picture frame • In a watertight jar in a pond

CAR JOURNEY GAMES

I SPY

Look around and choose an object for the other passengers to guess. Let them know the letter the object begins with by saying 'I spy with my little eye something beginning with ...' The first person to guess correctly takes the next turn.

SCISSORS, PAPER, STONE

Hold your right hand in a fist and get a friend to do the same. Count to three out loud and then, at the same time, each use your hand to mime either a pair of scissors (first two fingers held open), a piece of paper (a flat hand) or a stone (a fist). Scissors beat (cut) paper. Paper beats (covers) stone. Stone beats (blunts) scissors.

THE ALPHABET GAME

Choose a category such as 'things that smell bad', 'wild animals', or 'famous people', and think of an example to fit the chosen category for each letter of the alphabet.

FIRST TO 20

Each choose something to count: for example, yellow cars, Belgian lorries or squashed animals. The first to count 20 of their chosen category wins.

SING THE MILEAGE SONG

Substitute for 'X' the number of miles you have left to drive in the following song: 'X more miles to go, X more miles of sorrow, X more miles in this old car and we'll be there tomorrow.'

APOLOGIZE PROFUSELY FOR SINGING THE MILEAGE SONG

Say sorry over and over until you reach your destination.

EXTREME CHALLENGES

THE POLAR CHALLENGE
592-km (368-mile) trek
to the North Pole.
X-factor: Freezing conditions.

DAKAR MOTOR RALLY
9,000-km (5,600-mile) motor
race across North Africa.
X-factor: The Sahara
Desert.

VENDÉE GLOBE
37,000-km (23,000-mile)
non-stop solo sail
around the world.
X-factor: Storms.

DEATH VALLEY
ULTRA-MARATHON
217-km (135-mile) run across
America's Wild West.
X-factor: Soaring
temperatures.

TEXAS WATER SAFARI
Three-day 421-km (262-mile)
non-stop canoe race along
the Colorado River
to the Gulf of Mexico.
X-factor: Swirling currents.

WESTERN STATES
TRAIL RIDE
161-km (100-mile) 24-hour
horse race across the
Sierra Nevada Mountains.
X-factor: Saddle sores.

LA RUTA DE LOS
CONQUISTADORES
483-km (300-mile),
three-day mountain-bike
race in the Costa
Rican jungle.
X-factor: Two volcanoes.

SEAFARING SUPERSTITIONS

GOOD LUCK

Seeing a black cat before
setting sail

Placing a silver coin under
the masthead

Seeing a swallow

Dolphins swimming
alongside the ship

The feather of a wren killed
on New Year's Day

BAD LUCK

Crossing paths with a
redhead before setting sail

Looking back to port once
you have set sail

Setting sail on a Friday

Killing an albatross

Hearing church bells

Saying the word 'drowned'

Drowning

AVIATION LIGHT SIGNALS

If radio communication breaks down, air traffic control uses a light gun to signal messages to the aircraft.

Steady green...Cleared to land

Flashing green...Cleared to approach airport

Steady red..................................Continue circling, give way to other aircraft

Flashing red..Airport unsafe, do not land

Alternating red and green..............................Danger, continue current action with caution

---

> The word television comes from the Greek *tele* for 'far' and Latin *visio* for 'sight'.

IS THIS GO-KART MOVING?

Stare at the wheels of the go-kart below. Jiggle the book and see if you can make the wheels turn.

WHO'S WHO IN A FILM CREW

Producer...In charge of raising money

Director.....................Responsible for content of film and performances

Scriptwriter...Writes the screenplay

Location manager..Finds the right places to film

Grip..In charge of lighting and rigging

Dolly grip......................In charge of moving cameras on the dolly track

Gaffer..Head of the electrical department

Visual effects supervisor...Creates special effects

Foley artist...Creates and records sound effects

Best boy...Technical assistant

Swing gang................Team that makes last-minute changes to the set

ALMOST SURELY

In probability theory, the phrase 'almost surely' has a
precise meaning. It is an event that has zero probability
of not occurring – i.e. it is 'almost surely' going to happen,
even though it is still possible that it might not occur.

ACCIDENTALLY TASTY

CHOCOLATE CHIP COOKIES

In the 1930s, Ruth Wakefield, the owner of the Toll House Inn in Massachusetts, USA, sprinkled chocolate bits into her cookie mixture expecting them to melt. But the chocolate bits held their shape, and instead of making chocolate biscuits, she got butter biscuits full of chocolate chips.

CORNFLAKES

While working in a hospital in the US state of Michigan in 1884, the Kellogg brothers left a pot of wheat-flour mixture to stand too long. Wondering what would happen, they put the stale wheat through the rollers anyway. Instead of the usual long sheet of dough, they got flakes of wheat that they roasted and served to their patients. They were soon selling their tasty invention under the name 'Granose'.

CRÈME BRULÉE

Far from being a traditional French dish, it is said that crème brulée or 'burnt cream' originated in 17th-century England. Having accidentally scorched a bowl of custard sprinkled with sugar, the chef at Trinity College, part of Cambridge University, served up the caramelized offering as a new dish. At the university it is still known as 'Trinity College cream'.

PAGAN FESTIVALS

Yule.....................Marks the shortest day of the year, winter solstice

Imbolc...................Celebrates the lengthening of the days, 2 February

Ostara...Festival of spring, spring equinox

Beltane...............................Celebrates the onset of summer, 1 May

Litha....................Marks the longest day of the year, summer solstice

Lammas...Harvest festival, 1 August

Mabon...............................Festival of autumn, autumn equinox

Samhain........The beginning of the dark half of the year, 31 October

THE RICHTER SCALE

In 1935, the US seismologist (earthquake expert) Charles Richter developed a scale for measuring the strength of earthquakes, based on the magnitude of vibrations in the ground. Each level on the scale is ten times greater than the preceding one.

0 to 2...Detected by instruments, but not humans

3 to 4...Hanging lights sway, windows rattle

5...................At epicentre, objects fall off shelves and windows shatter

6...................Within 10 km (6 miles), chimneys crack and roof tiles fall

7............Within 100 km (60 miles), the ground cracks and pipes burst

8...........................Within 300 km (185 miles), buildings are destroyed

9...........................Within 1,000 km (620 miles), waves ripple the ground,

and buildings and bridges fall

VIKING NAMES

Bjorn Ironside • Eric Bloodaxe
Ivar the Boneless • Orvar-odd
Harold Bluetooth • Sigrid the Haughty
Sigurd Snake-eye • Halfdan the Black
Hrolf the Walker • Ingvar the Far-travelled

To work out your own Viking name, either:

1. Follow your first name with the word 'blood-' and the name of your favourite weapon. For example, if your name is Daniel and your favourite weapon is your super-strong thumb, your Viking name would be Daniel Bloodthumb.

OR:

2. Follow your first name with the word 'the' and then your most memorable quality – the more evil the better. For example, if your name is James and you are famous for your deadly erupting farts, your Viking name would be James the Eruptor.

HOW TO PLAY POOHSTICKS

First of all, you need to find a footbridge spanning running water. Gather your friends together at your chosen spot, and tell them to find a stick each. Make sure you can tell the sticks apart. How about attaching a different coloured ribbon to each one?

Line everyone up in a row on the bridge, so that the current is flowing towards them and underneath the bridge. Instruct each person to drop their stick on the count of three. When the sticks hit the water, rush over to the other side of the bridge to see whose stick emerges first.

A good tip when playing Poohsticks is to examine the stream or river before the competition. If possible, make sure you are in a position on the bridge to drop your stick in to the area of the river where the current is flowing fastest, and where it will avoid any obstacles, such as rocks or reeds.

MAGIC WORDS

Abracadabra • Hocus pocus • Open sesame

Izzy wizzy let's get busy • Alakazham

SPY SPEAK

What you say: 'It is raining in St. Petersburg.'
What you mean: 'The teacher is listening.'

What you say: 'The geese are heading north for the winter.'
What you mean: 'Meet me in the usual place after school.'

What you say: 'The roses are beautiful in Moscow this spring.'
What you mean: 'This is the person I fancy.'

What you say: 'The trains in Berlin always run on time.'
What you mean: 'Please cover for me.'

THE EQUATOR

The equator is an imaginary line that goes around the Earth halfway between the poles, dividing the planet into a northern and a southern hemisphere. It is about 40,000 km (25,000 miles) long.

There are 13 countries on the equator:

São Tomé and Príncipe • Gabon • Kenya

Republic of Maldives • Indonesia • Kiribati • Ecuador

Democratic Republic of Congo • The Republic of Congo

Uganda • Somalia • Colombia • Brazil

—————— HOW TO FIND ORION ——————

Orion is one of the largest constellations and was known by the Ancient Greeks as 'The Great Hunter'.

The constellation is home to the famous Orion Nebula, which is a collection of gas and dust which can be seen with the naked eye. You can see Orion wherever you are in the world.

The easiest way to find Orion is to look for the 'belt'. If you are in the northern hemisphere, look to the south and try to pick out three stars in a short, straight line.

If you imagine the constellation as the figure of a hunter, the Orion Nebula is the 'sword' that hangs from the belt you have located. To the lower left of the belt is the brightest star in the sky, known as the Dog Star, Sirius. Betelgeuse is the name of the orange-red star which appears above the belt, and to the left.

—————— BODILY FLUIDS ——————

Pus is made of dead bacteria and dead blood cells.

Bogeys are made mostly of sugars;
that is why they taste so nice.

You have 250,000 pores on your feet, which produce approximately half a pint (284 ml) of sweat every day.

You spray about 300 droplets of spit
a minute when you are talking.

—— CAT WORDS ——   —— RAT WORDS ——

Catalogue   Ratatouille
Catapult   Ratbag
Category   Rattle
Catastrophe   Ratatat
Catamaran   Ratify

POPCORN

Every kernel of popcorn contains a tiny amount of water. When a kernel is heated, this water turns to steam. The pressure grows until ... 'pop!' – the kernel explodes with a rush of steam. The kernel turns inside out and the inside expands like white foam.

The first popcorn was made by Native Americans and flavoured with herbs and spices. According to folklore the popping sound was made by angry corn spirits that burst out when the kernels became too hot to live in.

The average popping temperature for popcorn is 175°C (347°F).

A water content of 13.5 per cent produces the ideal pop.

Popcorn has been served in cinemas since 1912.

The average American consumes about 51 litres (11 gallons, or about 22 microwave popcorn bags) of popcorn every year.

Kernels that fail to pop are known as 'old maids'.

POPCORN FLAVOURS

Salt • Sugar • Caramel • Toffee • Curry

Cherry • Chilli • Cinnamon • Double chocolate

Coconut • Hot mustard • Nacho cheese

HALLOWEEN

In pagan times it was thought that the veil separating the worlds of humans and their gods became thin at the onset of winter. It was believed that on the festival of Samhain (31 October) the gods came to Earth and played evil tricks. Fearful people lit bonfires and made sacrifices in the hope that the gods would leave them alone during this perilous time. Today we call this festival Halloween.

HOW TO TALK LIKE A PIRATE – BEGINNERS

'Ahoy shipmates!'
'Hello everyone.'

'Aye!'
'Yes, I agree.'

'Aye aye!'
'I'm right on that!'

'Avast!'
'Stop!'

'Arrr!'
*Grunt used to fill
pauses in conversation.*

BEE COLONIES

A honeybee hive contains thousands of bees of three different types: the queen, the workers and the drones.

THE QUEEN
A specially nurtured female that emerges from the hive and mates with about 20 drones. She spends the next two years of her life laying eggs.

THE WORKERS
Females that develop from fertilized eggs to make the honey, build and guard the hive, tend the eggs, feed the larvae, and raise the next queen. Workers are sterile, and cannot reproduce.

THE DRONES
Stingless males bred from unfertilized eggs purely to mate with the queen. In the process of mating, their vital organs are ripped out and they die. Any drones that don't die in this way are massacred by the workers, or turfed out of the hive to starve or die of cold.

COUNTRY-FAIR SPORTS

JINGLING MATCH
A dozen blindfolded people move around within a roped-off ring. A man enters the ring without a blindfold, but with a bell around his neck and both hands tied behind him. The blindfolded men have to catch him.

SHIN KICKING
Athletes wearing iron-tipped boots kick each other in the shins. The first person to fall over twice loses.

FOOT WRESTLING
Two players lie on their backs on a wooden board with the soles of their feet touching. The object is to push the opponent off the board.

GREASY POLE
A greased telegraph pole is suspended over water with a flag at the furthest end. Players take it in turns to try to climb along the pole and reach the flag without falling into the water.

THE ABC OF LIFE-SAVING

A is for Airway.
Check it is open and not blocked.

B is for Breathing.
Make sure it is even and regular.

C is for Circulation.
Check for a pulse to make sure blood is circulating around the body.

REAL ROCK STAR REQUESTS

'I want a bowl of M&Ms with all the brown ones removed.'

'All my food must be wrapped in clear plastic.'

'I want the seven dwarves up here now!'

'My coffee always has to be stirred anti-clockwise.'

'I want my hotel napkins personalized with my initials.'

'I want a dimmer switch in my dressing room.'

'I want bunny rabbits and kittens backstage
to keep me company.'

SLEEPY ANIMALS

Koala..................................22 hours per day

Little brown bat....................19 hours per day

Python...............................18 hours per day

Tiger..................................16 hours per day

Three-toed sloth...................15 hours per day

Cat....................................12 hours per day

Humans..............................8 hours per day

Indian elephant.....................4 hours per day

Horse.................................3 hours per day

Giraffe...............................2 hours per day

A SONG THAT GETS ON EVERYBODY'S NERVES

'I know a song that gets on everybody's nerves.
I know a song that gets on everybody's nerves.
I know a song that gets on everybody's nerves.
And this is how it goes ...'
[Repeat forever]

THE WORLD'S COOLEST BUNGEE JUMPS

CLIFTON SUSPENSION BRIDGE (England)
The Oxford Dangerous Sports Club invented the modern bungee jump on 1 April 1978. The first ever bungee jump was from the 76-m (249-ft) Clifton Suspension Bridge.

BLOUKRANS RIVER BRIDGE (South Africa)
This is the world's highest commercial bungee jump. Jumpers experience a seven-second free fall from the 216-m (708-ft) bridge.

THE 'GOLDENEYE' DAM
(Switzerland-Italy border)
In the 1995 film *GoldenEye*, James Bond bungee-jumps over the edge of a dam in Russia. This dam is in fact on the Swiss-Italian border, but the stunt was genuine.

BORED OF BUNGEE JUMPS? TRY THESE!

BUNGEE DROP
This is the same as a bungee jump except that you cut the cord just before springing back up from the ground, and touch down safely.

THE CATAPULT
You start on the ground and the bungee cord is stretched from wherever it is fixed. When released, this pulls you up into the air at great speed.

BUNGEE TRAMPOLINE
You are suspended in a harness from bungee cords that let you jump much higher than you normally could on a trampoline.

BRIDGE SWING
You free-fall from a bridge and then swing backwards and forwards in a long, high-speed arc (instead of bouncing up and down as you would during a bungee jump).

A QUICK GUIDE TO WESTERN PHILOSOPHY

EXISTENTIALISM
Life has no deeper meaning so I am free to act as I choose. On the other hand, since life has no meaning, I might as well not bother doing anything.

MATERIALISM
Only physical things truly exist. Everything else, such as love or anger or a belief in God, can be explained in physical terms.

FATALISM
Everything that is going to happen is already decided and I have no free will. Since everything will happen the same, no matter what I do, I might as well do nothing.

RELATIVISM
There is no right and wrong, and no good and evil. There are only judgements that we agree on.

SOLIPSISM
I am real and so are my experiences, but I can't be sure that anything else exists.

EMPIRICISM
True knowledge comes through practical experience, not thought.

POSTMODERNISM
There is nothing that is true for the whole of humanity. We are therefore free to invent and practise our own philosophies.

INUIT WORDS FOR SNOW

Iñupiaq is a language spoken by Iñupiaq Inuits in Alaska. Here are some of their words for snow:

Aniuvak..A mound of packed snow

Apun..Fallen snow

Nutagaq...Fresh powder snow

Piqsiq...Wet snow

Pukak....................Granular snow formed under another layer

Qanattaaq...Overhanging snow

Qannik...Falling snow

Silliq...Crusty, hard snow

LEGALLY BLIND

A legally blind person has to stand 6 m (20 ft) away
from an object to see it with the same degree of clarity
as a normally sighted person can from 60 m (200 ft),
even when wearing the best glasses.

TRADITIONAL CAKES

Pumpkin pie..USA

Moon cake...China

Victoria sponge..England

Poppyseed cake..Poland

Pavlova...New Zealand

Lady fingers..France

Cheesecake..Ancient Greece

Black Forest gateau.....................................Germany

---

Due to the nature of infinity, an infinite number of monkeys
randomly hitting the keys of a typewriter will eventually
type out the complete works of William Shakespeare.

MISSING TREASURE

THE CROWN JEWELS OF MARIE ANTOINETTE

In 1792, the jewels of the beheaded French queen Marie Antoinette were stolen by revolutionaries. The Sancy Diamond and French Blue Diamond were never recovered.

KING JOHN'S TREASURE

The King of England lost his treasure, including the Crown Jewels, when horses pulling a carriage containing the treasure got disorientated in a swirling fog. They dragged the treasure carriage into a murky stretch of water.

NAZI GOLD

During the Second World War, Nazis in Germany looted foreigners' treasure. Gold was transferred into top-secret Swiss banks and never heard of again.

THE KNIGHTS' TEMPLAR TREASURE

This powerful order of medieval knights were thought to have been the guardians of the Holy Grail. To this day the Grail's whereabouts allegedly remains a closely guarded secret.

Chinese gooseberries come from New Zealand.

HOW TO TALK LIKE A PIRATE – ADVANCED

'The Sun be over the yardarm, 'tis time for victuals, and smartly, me hearty!'
'It's getting late – hurry up with dinner, I'm starving, mate!'

'Let's see what's crawled out of the bunghole.'
'Let's see what's for dinner.'

'Bring me a noggin of rum, now, won't you, matey?'
'Can I have a drink?'

'The cat's out of the bag, the wind's gone out of me sails, and I'll be swinging from the yardarm afore eight bells.'
'I'm in big trouble.'

——— NOT-SO-SECRET DIARIES ———

DIARY OF A WIMPY KID
Written by Jeff Kinney,
a diary (there are now nine
diaries) about the life, problems
and misadventures of middle-
schooler Greg Heffley.

THE DIARY
OF SAMUEL PEPYS
This 17th-century Londoner
wrote his diaries in a code
that wasn't cracked until
long after his death. He
wrote about the things he
saw first-hand, including the
Great Fire of London and
public executions.

THE DIARY OF
ANNE FRANK
Anne Frank was a Jewish
Dutch girl who went into
hiding from the Nazis during
the Second World War.
She kept a diary for the two
years that she spent in a
secret annex of a house.

CAPTAIN SCOTT'S JOURNAL
Robert Falcon Scott
kept a diary of his team's
expedition to the South
Pole in 1912. He and four
others died shortly after
reaching the Pole.

——— KNOCK, KNOCK. WHO'S THERE? ———

Major.....................Major look, Major stare, Major lose your underwear

Boo...Don't cry. It's only a joke

Nunya...Nunya business!

Al.....................Al bust this door down if you don't let me in

Amanda.....................................A man dat wants to come in

Toby.........................Toby or not Toby, that is the question

Atch...Bless you!

Albert.........................Albert you don't know who I am

Elma.....................Elma-ny more knock, knock jokes can you take?

> The worst Viking vengeance was known as the 'Blood-
> Red Eagle'. The enemy's back was cut open, his ribs
> were pulled from his spine and his lungs were removed.

WHAT'S THE USE?

Silent alarm clock	Waterproof sponge
Double-sided playing cards	Fireproof matches
Inflatable anchor	Glow-in-the-dark sunglasses
Smooth sandpaper	Inflatable dart board
Non-stick sticky tape	Helicopter ejector seat

OXYMORONS

Oxymorons are words that are used together
that have contradictory meanings. They don't make
any sense, but they make complete sense.

Living dead

Seriously funny

Same difference

Virtual reality

Almost exactly

Deafening silence

Clearly confused

SIXTH SENSE

Intuition...A gut feeling about something

Déjà vu.....................The feeling of having seen something before

Telepathy.............The ability to pass thoughts from person to person

Medium......................Someone who can sense the presence of spirits

Visionary.......A person who can see into the future through dreams

Mind-reading................................Tuning in to another person's thoughts

NATURAL HAIRSTYLES

Widow's peak............................V-shaped point in middle of forehead

Cowlick..........................Swirl of unruly hair that can't be combed down

Crown...............................A whorl of hair at the centre of the scalp

Double crown.................Two whorls of hair at the centre of the scalp

HOW FAR CAN YOU SEE?

ON A CLEAR DAY

As far as the Sun, 150 million km (93 million miles) away

ON A CLEAR NIGHT

As far as the Andromeda Galaxy, 2 million light years away
(one light year is 9.5 million million km (nearly
6 million million miles))

WITH THE BEST TELESCOPE

14 billion light years away

The fastest speed ever reached on a
skateboard was 100.6 kph (62.5 mph). The
skater was Gary Hardwick of California, USA.

HEALING CRYSTALS

Amethyst..Peace and harmony

Carnelian..Focus

Citrine...Mental clarity

Quartz...Energy and healing

Amber..Digestion and reproduction

Tiger's eye..Well-being and confidence

Tourmaline...Purity and protection

——— ALLEGED MERMAID SIGHTINGS ———

ENGLAND, 1167
A merman was
washed up onto the
beach at Orford,
Suffolk. He was kept
in Orford Castle for
six months before
escaping back
into the sea.

POLAND, 1531
A mermaid caught by fishermen in the Baltic Sea was sent
to the King of Poland. She died after three days in captivity.

CEYLON, 1560
Seven merpeople were spotted by passengers on board
a boat bound for India, off the west coast of Ceylon (now
Sri Lanka). Witnesses included the Viceroy of Goa.

IRELAND, 1819
A young mermaid was caught off the Irish coast. She was the
size of a ten-year-old child with long hair and dark eyes. A boy
shot at her with a gun and she disappeared back into the sea.

——— THE YOSEMITE SYSTEM OF MOUNTAINEERING ———

The Yosemite system of mountaineering grades the difficulty
of climbing routes.

Class 1...Hiking

Class 2...................Simple scrambling with occasional use of hands

Class 3.......................Scrambling with occasional aid of a rope

Class 4..............Simple climbing with exposure and possible fatal falls

Class 5..Technical free climbing

Class 6...................Artificial or aid climbing; for example, climbing
a rope up a sheer face with no holds

DO-IT-YOURSELF HUMAN BEINGS

GOLEM

In Jewish folklore, a golem was a human-like creature made of clay and brought to life by a holy man. The golem could not speak and would perform tasks for the holy man. Often he would cause trouble by taking a task too literally.

FRANKENSTEIN'S MONSTER

In Mary Shelley's novel *Frankenstein*, the Swiss scientist Dr Frankenstein creates a monster out of body parts taken from local graveyards and dissecting rooms. The monster wreaks havoc after he is shunned by the horrified doctor.

HOMUNCULUS

According to the 15th-century Austrian alchemist Paracelsus, a homunculus was a human-like being made in the warmth of horse manure and nourished by human blood. Marvellous creatures such as pygmies, woodsprites and giants were all homunculi.

PINOCCHIO

In the children's story by the Italian author Carlo Collodi, a wooden puppet made by the childless carpenter Geppetto comes to life. After proving his worth, the puppet, called Pinocchio, is magically turned into a real boy.

FEATS OF GREAT STRENGTH

Performing one-fingered press-ups
Ripping up a telephone directory
Bending a steel bar
Breaking metal chains
Lifting a car
Pushing a bus with your head
Pulling a Boeing 747

THE COLOUR OF NOISE

If sound waves are translated into light waves, different sounds appear as different colours.

SOUNDS WAVES   LIGHT WAVES

TV static, urban traffic..White

Rushing water or ocean surf...Pink

Subway train, noisy air-conditioning system...........................Red

Roomful of five-year-olds playing recorders........................Orange

Piercing hiss..Blue

Random footsteps...Brown

Natural background noise...Green

Silence..Black

> Identical twins usually die within
> three years of each other.

UNLIKELY PARTNERSHIPS

THE CLOWN FISH AND THE SEA ANEMONE

The clown fish is immune to the anemone's stinging tentacles. It keeps the anemone's tentacles clean and in return is protected from predators.

THE ANT AND THE CATERPILLAR

Some Australian caterpillars have special glands that produce a honey-like liquid that ants like to drink. In return, the ants protect the defenceless caterpillar from parasites.

THE PILOT FISH AND THE SHARK

Tiny pilot fish swim into sharks' mouths and nibble away any rotting food caught between the sharks' teeth. Sharks rarely eat these swimming toothpicks, and instead help them by scaring off would-be predators.

THE KNIGHTS' CODE

Rescue damsels in distress.

Love your country.

Defend your monarch.

Respect your fellow knights.

Never refuse a challenge.

Don't hide from your enemies.

Live honourably and fight for glory.

Give to the poor.

Protect the weak.

Stand up against injustice.

Don't tell lies.

Always finish what you begin.

HOW TO RECOGNIZE A WITCH

Throughout history, people all over the world believed in and were afraid of witches. Instructions on how to recognize one were written down and passed on from one generation to the next. Here are some of the things that were thought to be proof that somebody was a witch:

Witches are not able to shed tears.

Witches cannot drown.

Witches can change themselves into hares. The only way to kill them when they are in this form is with a silver bullet.

Any animals or crops near a witch's house will eventually become diseased and die.

A witch will have a familiar, a devoted animal that is never far from her side – often a black cat.

INTERESTING BRIDGES

BRIDGE OF SIGHS, VENICE, ITALY
Prisoners crossed this bridge before being taken to their cells.
It is said they would sigh as they took their last view of Venice.

LONDON BRIDGE, LONDON, ENGLAND
Until 1750 this was the only bridge over the River Thames.
Heads of traitors were placed on spikes above the
southern gate of the bridge.

MILLAU BRIDGE, MASSIF CENTRAL MOUNTAINS, FRANCE
343 m (1,125 ft) tall at its highest point,
this bridge is taller than the Eiffel Tower.

THE FORTH RAIL BRIDGE, QUEENSFERRY, SCOTLAND
This Victorian bridge is so long that, until recent developments
in paint technology, it had to be continuously painted – as soon
as the people painting it had got to the end, it was time
to start at the beginning again!

GOLDEN GATE BRIDGE, SAN FRANCISCO, USA
When it was built in 1937, at 2,737 m long, this was the largest
suspension bridge in the world. Today the Akashi Kaikyo Bridge
in Japan holds that title, measuring 3,911 m.

MATHEMATICAL BRIDGE, CAMBRIDGE, ENGLAND
Rumoured to have been designed by Sir Isaac Newton
without the use of nuts or bolts to hold the wood together.
According to legend, students dismantled the bridge one
night, but were unable to put it back together. It was
then rebuilt using nuts and bolts.

COOL GADGETS

Bulletproof jacket • Lock-picking kit • Micro-tracers

Grappling hook • Smart watch • Smokescreen pellets

Anti-puncture bike tyres • Smart glasses

Anti-gravity hovering skateboard

Super-strong rope contained in a yo-yo

THE WORLD'S SIMPLEST CARD TRICK

1.   Shuffle the deck in front of a friend.

2.   Secretly peek at the card on the bottom and remember it.

3.   Ask your friend to pick a card, any card, from the deck and look at it carefully without showing you.

4.   Cut the cards – take the top half of the deck in your left hand and the bottom half in your right hand.

5.   Hold out the left-hand pile and tell your friend to put their card on top of it.

6.   Put the cards from your right hand on top of the pile.

7.   You can now work through the pack, card by card, until you come to the card originally on the bottom of the pack. Your friend's card is the next one, but go past it so that it looks like you've missed it.

8.   Return to the correct card and sit back as your friend stares at you in awe and amazement.

HOW LOUD IS A DECIBEL?

0 decibels...Threshold of hearing

10...Human breathing

15...Whisper

80...Vacuum cleaner

90...Loud factory (harmful)

120...Rock concert

130...Train horn

150...Rifle firing

180...Blue whale humming

250.................................Inside a tornado (death to humans)

A WARNING TO PIRATES

The notorious British pirate Captain Kidd was hanged at Execution Dock in London on 23 May 1701. On the first attempt, the rope broke, so Kidd was strung up and hanged again. His body was suspended in the sea and left for the tide to wash over it three times. Then it was painted in tar, bound in chains and hung up in a metal cage. His rotting corpse served as a warning to pirates sailing in and out of London.

SWITCHING ON A LIGHT

The speed of light is approximately 300,000 km per second (186,000 miles per second). If you could slow this down to 1 m per second you would be able to see the way shadows are gradually chased away when you turn on a light:

You flick the light switch. For a while nothing happens.

After a few seconds the light bulb gradually begins to light up, but the room remains completely dark.

Slowly a sphere of light begins to spread around the bulb, creating a halo effect. Gradually the sphere of light expands to fill the room.

The room is now completely illuminated, apart from the shadows which remain pitch black.

Light bouncing off the walls begins to fill the shadows, and eventually they start to lighten.

You switch off the light. The shadows are the last areas to return to pitch black.

ANIMAL RECORDS

Largest animal..Blue whale 33.5 m (110 ft), 209 tons

Largest land animal.............African bush elephant 3.9 m (13 ft), 8 tons

Tallest animal..Giraffe 5.8 m (19 ft)

Largest reptile........Saltwater crocodile 4.9 m (16 ft), 522 kg (1,150 lb)

Longest snake.................................Reticulated python 8-10 m (26-32 ft)

Longest animal...Whale shark 12.7 m (41.8 ft)

Largest bird..Ostrich 2.7 m (9 ft), 156.5 kg (345 lb)

Largest insect...Stick insect 38 cm (15 in)

Fastest animal..................................Peregrine falcon 386 kph (240 mph)

Fastest land animal...Cheetah 112 kph (70 mph)

Fastest insect...Dragonfly 57 kph (36 mph)

The world record for ripping up telephone directories is held by Ed Charon of the USA. On 14 September 2006, he ripped up 56 directories from top to bottom in three minutes.

THE GAME

The Game is a mental game. The aim of The Game is to forget that you are playing it. As many players as you want can play. Players only need to be aware of a few simple rules:

1. To know of The Game's existence is to play The Game.
2. To realize you have thought of The Game is to lose The Game.
3. When you lose, you must immediately announce, 'I have lost The Game.'
4. If anyone present asks 'What is The Game?' you must explain these rules.
5. Other players of The Game who are present when you announce that you have lost have a 30-minute grace period in which to forget about The Game before they also lose.
6. It is not possible to know that you have won The Game, only to have won it and remain ignorant of the fact.

THE HIGHEST MOUNTAINS ON MARS

Olympus Mons.................................27 km (16.8 miles)

Ascraeus Mons...............................11 km (6.8 miles)

Arsia Mons.......................................9 km (5.6 miles)

Pavonis Mons..................................7 km (4.3 miles)

Alba Patera......................................3 km (1.9 miles)

The highest mountain on Earth is Mount Everest, which is 8.85 km (5.5 miles) high.

RUSSIAN SPACE DOGS

Laika • Belka • Strelaka
Chernushka • Veterok
Ugolyok

AMERICAN SPACE MONKEYS

Albert • Gordo • Able
Baker • Sam • Bonny
Scatback

SUPERHEROES YOU PROBABLY DON'T KNOW

ULTRAMAN (Japan)
40-m- (132-ft-) tall alien from
Nebula M78. He can fly
at seven times the speed
of sound and can only
spend three minutes
on Earth at a time.

STIG (Canada)
An undead spirit, Stig was
attacked by demons and
woke to find himself in Hell.
Mistaken for Satan in disguise,
he became leader of the
Underworld, with the
ability to send bolts of
fire from his hands.

EL BULBO (Mexico)
Brought to life when a
spell was cast on the
bulbs in a television set,
El Bulbo is a superhero
who fights his arch-rival
and fellow light bulb Adolfo.
He can fly, grow to an
enormous size and
fire destructive rays.

NAGRAJ (India)
Microscopic snakes living
in his bloodstream give him
superhuman strength, a
venomous bite and snakes
that shoot out of his wrists.

Scientists think it likely that the universe
was created 13.7 billion years ago.

REVOLUTIONS

AMERICAN REVOLUTION
The 13 colonies of America broke away from Great Britain
and became a republic of united states, 1775-83

FRENCH REVOLUTION
Overthrow of the French monarchy and aristocracy
and the establishment of a French republic, 1789-99

RUSSIAN REVOLUTION
Abdication of Tsar Nicholas II and the
establishment of Soviet Union, 1917

VELVET REVOLUTION
Bloodless overthrow of Communist government
in Czechoslovakia, 1989

FENCING TERMS

A bout...A fencing match

Salute...............A courteous gesture at the start and finish of a bout

Allee!...The command to begin

Parry...A defensive stroke

Riposte...A counter-attack after a parry

Esquive...............Ducking or side-stepping to avoid being hit

Pattinando...A lunge

Coulé..A glide

Prise de fer..Taking the opponent's blade

Finale.....................The last move in a series of attacking actions

PANGRAMS

Pangrams are sentences that contain every letter of
the alphabet at least once.

The quick brown fox jumps over the lazy dog.

The five boxing wizards jump quickly.

Five or six jet planes zoomed quickly by the tower.

FREE-RUNNING MOVES

Free running is usually practised in urban areas and is a way of moving through the environment fluidly. Free runners use a series of vaults, jumps and athletic movements to pass through, over and under everyday obstacles such as stairs, rails and walls.

Wall climb..Scaling a vertical surface

Underbar....................................Jumping or swinging through a gap

Gap jump...................................Jumping from one location to another

Turn vault.................................Vaulting to the other side of an object

Tic tac.......................................Kicking off one surface to clear another

Rail precision...............................Jumping from one rail to another

Cat balance.......................Running on hands and feet along a rail or narrow surface

THE FIVE KINGDOMS OF LIVING THINGS

Monerans	Organisms with simple cell structures; for example, bacteria.
Protists	Simple organisms with nuclei and other complex cell structures; for example, some algae.
Fungi	Primitive plants that decompose dead plant and animal matter; for example, mushrooms and yeast.
Plants	Multicellular organisms, usually with cell walls composed mainly of cellulose. Plants typically use sunlight as an energy source, and convert light energy, water and carbon dioxide into glucose, oxygen and water through a process called photosynthesis.
Animals	Multicellular organisms that feed on other organisms. Almost all animals can respond to changes in their environment by moving all or part of their bodies.

A KNIGHTLY TOURNAMENT

JOUST
Knights on horseback charge at each other with long lances under their arms. The aim is to knock your opponent off his horse.

MELÉE A PIED
Knights fight on foot with blunted swords. You win if you strike your opponent three times.

ARCHERY
Knights shoot 12 arrows at the centre of a target, scoring points for accuracy. The best shot wins.

WRESTLING
Knights fight unarmed and the winner is decided by the best of five throws.

REALLY STUPID

A woman in Texas, USA, had bought a new car and wanted to check out the size of the boot. She asked her family members to shut her inside it, then realized she was still holding the keys.

While out hunting in Arizona, USA, a man accidentally shot himself in the leg. To try to attract the attention of someone who could rescue him, he fired his gun a second time. Unfortunately he shot himself in the other leg.

A shopkeeper in Texas, USA, accepted a fake $100 bill even though it was over a foot long.

Some British soldiers, who were standing in for the fire service during a strike in 1978, were called to help an old lady rescue her cat from a tree. Mission accomplished, she invited them in for some tea and biscuits. Afterwards, the soldiers waved goodbye, got in their vehicle and ran over the cat.

TRACKING FOOTPRINTS

Grizzly bear	Duck	Beaver
Wild pig	Hedgehog	Monster

WAVE HEIGHT SCALE

Glassy...0 m (0 ft)

Rippled..0.3–0.6 m (1–2 ft)

Choppy..0.6–1.2 m (2–4 ft)

Very rough...4–6 m (13–20 ft)

Mid-ocean storm waves.....................................6–9 m (20–30 ft)

Extreme waves...15–30 m (50–100 ft)

Freak waves...30 m+ (100 ft+)

THE WORLD'S MOST DANGEROUS ANIMALS

POLAR BEAR

Found only in the Arctic, the polar bear is the largest land carnivore, and is twice the size of a tiger. It hunts both on land and in the sea, camouflaged white against the snow. When food is scarce, polar bears may kill and eat humans.

GREAT WHITE SHARK

Up to 6 m (20 ft) long and weighing over 2,000 kg (4,400 lb), the great white shark is the world's largest predatory fish. Great whites ambush their prey by swimming up from the bottom of the sea. They have extra rows of teeth behind their main ones that are constantly growing. Their teeth are retractable, like a cat's claws.

BOX JELLYFISH

Also known as the sea wasp, this cube-shaped jellyfish is only found in tropical seas. Its tentacles unleash fast-working venom that can shut down a human victim's heart and lungs in as little as three minutes. Kills more people every year than any other sea creature.

FUNNEL-WEB SPIDER

The world's most deadly spider comes from Australia, where it likes to live in cool, sheltered habitats. The males are known to bite aggressively and repeatedly. Death can occur any time from 15 minutes to three days after the bite.

INLAND TAIPAN SNAKE

Found in Central Australia, this snake has 12-mm- (0.5-in-) long fangs. It has the most lethal venom in the world, and one bite contains enough poison to kill several adult humans.

KOMODO DRAGON

The largest lizard in the world, the Komodo dragon hunts live prey on the island of Komodo in Indonesia. Deadly bacteria in the dragon's mouth quickly kill a bitten victim.

KILLER BEES

These extremely aggressive bees have a tendency to swarm. They have a high proportion of soldier bees that guard their hive, and pursue and sting perceived threats over long distances.

REAL CRAYON COLOURS

Magenta	Tan	Sea green
Pink sherbert	Wheat	Aquamarine
Crimson	Moccasin	Turquoise
Tomato	Almond	Cyan
Coral	Khaki	Teal
Salmon	Dandelion	Azure
Indian red	Lemon yellow	Sky blue
Fire brick	Gold	Navy
Maroon	Spring green	Midnight blue
Chocolate	Lawn green	Slate blue
Sienna	Lime	Cornflower blue
Sunset orange	Olive	Royal blue
Apricot	Forest	Steel blue
Goldenrod	Jungle green	Orchid

TECTONIC PLATES

The Earth's crust is made up of slabs of rock, known as tectonic plates, that are in constant motion.

African Plate	Juan de Fuca Plate
Antarctic Plate	Nazca Plate
Arabian Plate	North American Plate
Australian Plate	Pacific Plate
Caribbean Plate	Philippine Plate
Cocos Plate	Scotia Plate
Eurasian Plate	South American Plate
Indian Plate	

SERVING PLATES

Plates from which food is served or eaten.

Ashet
Dinner plate
Paper plate
Platter
Saucer
Side plate
Spinning plate
Trencher

THE OFFICIAL ROUTE TO DRACULA'S CASTLE

Day One: Catch the 11:36 pm overnight train from Munich in Bavaria to the Austrian capital Vienna, arriving at 6:10 am.

Day Two: After breakfasting in Vienna, take the early train to the Hungarian capital Budapest. There, catch a connecting train, arriving at nightfall in the Transylvanian town of Klausenburgh, also known as Cluj-Napoca. Stay the night at the Hotel Royale.

Day Three: Take the 11:27 am train to the northern Transylvanian city of Bistritz, also known as Bistrita. Arrive at lunchtime and stay at the Golden Krone Hotel, recommended by Count Dracula.

Day Four: Accept the crucifix given to you by the fearful hotelier when he discovers you are travelling to Dracula's Castle. Take the early-morning stagecoach to Bukovinia, on the north-eastern slopes of the Carpathian Mountains of Transylvania.

Day Five: At precisely midnight you will be dropped on the Borgo Pass, a lonely road that runs into the heart of the mountains. After a terrifying wait in the dark, a horseman will meet you and take you through a wolf-infested forest and blizzarding snow to Dracula's Castle.

ANIMALS THAT GIVE BIRTH TO CALVES

Buffalos • Elephants • Cows • Giraffes • Hippopotamuses
Moose • Camels • Antelopes • Elk • Whales • Dolphins

FAMOUS EQUATIONS

THE DEFINITION OF PI

Pi (π) is the ratio of the length of a circle's outer edge (circumference) to the distance across its centre (diameter). It is always the same, regardless of the size of the circle, and is roughly equal to 3.141592653.

$$\pi = \frac{c}{d}$$

π = pi
c = circumference of the circle
d = diameter of the circle

EINSTEIN'S THEORY OF RELATIVITY

Albert Einstein discovered that when an object has a mass (weight), it has an amount of energy related to that mass. The following equation works on the principle that the resting energy of an object is equal to its mass multiplied by the square of the speed of light:

$$E = mc^2$$

E = energy
m = mass
c = the speed of light

NEWTON'S GRAVITY LAW

Every object which has mass (weight) also has a gravitational pull. The larger the object, the stronger the pull. Every object, therefore, attracts every other object with a gravitational force that is proportional to each of their masses and the distance between them:

$$F = \frac{Gm_1m_2}{d^2}$$

F = force of gravitational attraction between two masses (m_1 and m_2)
G = gravitational constant (the force of gravity that is constantly present)
d = distance between the two masses

PYTHAGORAS'S THEOREM

In a right-angled triangle, the sum of the squares of the two shortest sides is equal to the square of the longest side:

$$a^2 + b^2 = c^2$$

a = short side of a right-angled triangle
b = other short side of a right-angled triangle
c = long side of a right-angled triangle

—— TIGHTROPE FEATS OF THE GREAT BLONDIN ——

The Great Blondin was the greatest daredevil ever to cross the Niagara Falls. On 30 June 1859 he walked on a tightrope over the Falls. When he got to the centre, he lowered a rope to a boat below, pulled up a bottle and sat down on his tightrope for a drink. He went on to perform the following amazing feats over the huge waterfall:

Cooking an omelette.

Riding a bicycle.

Doing a backwards somersault.

Walking with his hands and feet tied.

Walking blindfolded.

Pushing a wheelbarrow.

Carrying his manager on his back.

—————— HOW FAST IS STANDING STILL? ——————

The Earth is spinning around the Sun at approximately 112,000 kph (70,000 mph). Meanwhile, the solar system is travelling through space at 273 km per second (170 miles per second).

———— HOW MANY TO CHANGE A LIGHT BULB? ————

Owls...None. Owls aren't afraid of the dark

Martians...One and a half

Monkeys....................Three. One to change the light bulb, and two to throw bananas at each other

Poltergeists...........................Two. One to hold the light bulb and the other to twist the room around

STREET ART YOU CAN DO

Do five press-ups and have a friend count really loudly:
'996, 997, 998, 999, 1,000!'

Juggle uncooked eggs but keep dropping them.

Follow passers-by and impersonate the way they walk.

Sing out of tune through a traffic cone.

Talk to an imaginary person trapped down a grate.

Stand on a box and clear your throat as if you are about
to sing. Then clear your throat some more, and just
keep on clearing your throat.

Pretend you have jelly legs, and keep wobbling and falling
over and getting up and falling over again.

Draw ugly portraits of passers-by.

BAD LUCK AT THE THEATRE

Whistling or clapping backstage.

Saying *'Macbeth'*. (Instead, say 'The Scottish play.')

Wishing someone 'Good luck'. (Instead, say 'Break a leg.')

Turning off the light when the stage is not in use.

MAGICAL BEASTS IN HARRY POTTER BOOKS

HIPPOGRIFF
Beast of the air and of the ground, it has the head and wings of a giant eagle and the body of a horse. A stickler for the formalities of good manners, the hippogriff will be irritable if bows are not exchanged by way of greeting.

CENTAUR
Supremely intelligent being with the head and torso of a human and the body of a horse. Equally mistrustful of muggles and wizards, they live in deep forests.

HUNGARIAN HORNTAIL
Scaly, black dragon with yellow eyes. Frequent jets of flame are fired from its jaws and a blow from its spiked tail can be deadly.

WEREWOLF
When the Moon is full, this otherwise perfectly reasonable human turns into a bloodthirsty beast. The curse is caught from the bite of another werewolf, and there is no known cure. Werewolves are to be pitied, but not at close range on the night of a full Moon.

DOXY
Tiny, winged creature with four legs, four arms and a thick covering of black fur. They have venomous teeth and a deadly bite.

BASILISK
Venomous-fanged serpent with a deadly stare. Illegally produced by hatching a chicken's egg under a toad.

THE THREE OFFICIAL TYPES OF FREAK WAVE

WALL OF WATER
A wave that is preceded by a deep trough known as a 'hole in the sea' and travels up to 10 km (6 miles) through the ocean.

THREE SISTERS
Groups of three huge waves.

GIANT STORM WAVE
A single wave that builds to up to four times the normal height of a storm wave, then collapses after a few seconds.

ANIMAL DEFENCES

BADGERS
The skin on a badger's bottom is so baggy that if a predator gets its teeth into it, the badger is able to twist round and bite back.

RABBITS
A rabbit's eyes are set on the sides of its head. This increases the rabbit's field of vision and allows it to keep watch for predators, even while eating.

IO MOTHS
When threatened, these moths pull back their upper wings to reveal markings like a pair of eyes. This startles the attacker and gives the moth time to escape.

PUFFER FISH
These unusual fish can inflate themselves to several times their normal size by swallowing water or air.

HEDGEHOGS
When threatened by predators, hedgehogs roll up into a ball of prickles.

SKUNKS
Skunks spray a sticky and foul-smelling fluid at predators. The stench is strong enough to put off even the hardiest bear.

HOMONYMS

Homonyms are words that sound the same, but are spelt differently and have different meanings.

Carat - Carrot

Ate - Eight

Quay - Key

Wait - Weight

Dear - Deer

Knight - Night

Plain - Plane

Some - Sum

For - Four

You - Ewe

Pail - Pale

Scent - Cent

EVERYDAY CONUNDRUMS

CATCH-22
Sometimes called a vicious circle, a Catch-22 is a situation in which you have to do one thing to achieve another, but you can't achieve the first thing until you've achieved the second:

'I can't make money from washing cars until I've bought the equipment I need, but I can't buy the equipment I need until I've made some money from washing cars.'

MORTON'S FORK
A choice between two equally unpleasant alternatives:

'You can do your homework first and then clean your bedroom, or you can clean your bedroom first and then do your homework.'

HOBSON'S CHOICE
An apparently free choice that is really no choice at all:

'You can have either of these two chocolates, as long as I can have that one.'

FAMOUS NUMBERS

007..James Bond

666...The number of the devil

2000..The second millennium, or Y2K

9-11......................The date of the terrorist attacks on New York in 2001

180......................The highest possible score in the game of darts

13...Unlucky number

365...Days in a year (except leap years)

299,792,458.............................The speed of light in metres per second

$9^3/_4$.........................The train platform from which the Hogwart's Express departs in the Harry Potter books

80.........................The number of days it takes to go around the world in Jules Verne's novel *Around The World In Eighty Days*

ASSASSINATED LEADERS

MOHANDAS K. GANDHI

A pacifist campaigner for Indian independence, Gandhi was shot three times by his enemy Nathuram Godse on 30 January 1948.

ARCHDUKE FRANZ FERDINAND

Franz Ferdinand was the heir to the throne of Austro-Hungary. His assassination by Gavrilo Princip on 28 June 1914 sparked the First World War.

ABRAHAM LINCOLN

This President of the United States of America was assassinated on 14 April 1865 while watching a theatre performance. The assassin was John Wilkes Booth, who shot the President in the back of the head.

JOHN FITZGERALD KENNEDY

When this President of the United States of America was shot in the head on 22 November 1963, a man called Lee Harvey Oswald was accused. Many people believe that Oswald was either framed or part of a larger conspiracy.

JULIUS GAIUS CAESAR

On 15 March 44 BC, the Roman Emperor Julius Caesar was stabbed 23 times as the entered he senate. The assassination was carried out by a conspiracy of Roman senators, one of whom was Caesar's friend Brutus.

THE MINERAL HARDNESS SCALE

The Mohs scale is a system for classifying mineral hardness. Each mineral can make a scratch in those below it in the scale.

10. Diamond (hardest)
9. Corundum
8. Topaz
7. Quartz
6. Orthoclase

5. Apatite
4. Fluorite
3. Calcite
2. Gypsum
1. Talc (softest)

STAR SIGNS

SIGN	SYMBOL	ELEMENT	DATES
Aries	Ram	Fire	21 March-20 April
Taurus	Bull	Earth	21 April-21 May
Gemini	Twins	Air	22 May-21 June
Cancer	Crab	Water	22 June-22 July
Leo	Lion	Fire	23 July-23 Aug.
Virgo	Virgin	Earth	24 Aug-23 Sept.
Libra	Scales	Air	24 Sept-23 Oct.
Scorpio	Scorpion	Water	24 Oct-22 Nov.
Sagittarius	Archer	Fire	23 Nov-21 Dec.
Capricorn	Goat	Earth	22 Dec-20 Jan.
Aquarius	Water Carrier	Air	21 Jan-19 Feb.
Pisces	Fish	Water	20 Feb-20 March

ARIES - Energetic and enthusiastic but can be blunt.

TAURUS - Confident and artistic but can be unforgiving.

GEMINI - Talkative and charming but can be careless.

CANCER - Sensitive, kind and loyal but can be moody.

LEO - Sociable and generous but can be boastful.

VIRGO - Dependable and loyal but can be shy.

LIBRA - Balanced and helpful but can be indecisive.

SCORPIO - Determined and fearless but can be spiteful.

SAGITTARIUS - Optimistic and energetic but can be impulsive.

CAPRICORN - Loyal and humorous but can be over-sensitive.

AQUARIUS - Inquisitive and precise but can be stubborn.

PISCES - Imaginative and agreeable, but can over-exaggerate.

BIKES

Quadracycle • Penny farthing • Unicycle • Tandem
Exercise bike • Racing bike • Mountain bike • BMX

THE OFFICIAL RULES OF THE 'WORLD CHERRY PIT-SPITTING CHAMPIONSHIP'

1. Each cherry is put in the mouth whole and the flesh eaten before spitting the pit. The pit is the stone in the middle of the cherry.

2. The longest of three spits is recorded. If a pit is swallowed, that spit is forfeited.

3. No foreign objects may be held in the mouth that might give an advantage in spitting the pit.

4. No popping the cheeks. The spitter's hands must remain below the shoulders.

5. Contestants' feet may not touch or cross the foul line.

    The longest recorded spit is 28.5 m (93 ft 6½ in).

An anaconda snake can eat a 2-m- (6ft-7in-) long crocodile.

CULTURAL SYMBOLS

COUNTRY	ANIMAL	FOOD
Germany	Black eagle	Sauerkraut
USA	Bald eagle/Bison	Hamburger
England	Lion/Bulldog	Fish and chips
Wales	Red dragon	Laver bread
Australia	Kangaroo	Barbecue
France	Rooster	Frogs' legs
Scotland	Red lion	Haggis
Spain	Bull	Paella/Tapas
Russia	Eagle/Bear	Borscht
Canada	Beaver	Maple syrup

THE STORY OF WEAPONS

2,500,000 BC	Stone tools first used
6,000 BC	Metal spears first thrown
2,000 BC	Celtic tribes fight using horse-drawn chariots
400 BC	Ancient Greeks use ballistas (giant bolt throwers)
AD 950	Chinese invent gunpowder
1128	Chinese first use cannons
1400	Shotguns first used
1914-18	First World War - tanks first used instead of horses
1939-45	Second World War - assault rifles first used
1945	Allies use the first atomic bombs against Japan

SHOOTING STARS

METEOROID
Space debris of all shapes and sizes

METEOR
The glowing trail of burning gas that occurs when a meteoroid enters a planet's atmosphere and heats up

METEORITE
A meteoroid that hits the Earth

FAMOUS BEGINNINGS

'Once there were four children whose names were Peter, Susan, Edmund and Lucy.'
The Lion, the Witch and the Wardrobe by C. S. Lewis

'Alice was beginning to get very tired of sitting by her sister on the bank, and of having nothing to do: once or twice she had peeped into the book her sister was reading, but it had no pictures or conversations in it, "and what is the use of a book," thought Alice, "without pictures or conversations?"'
Alice's Adventures in Wonderland by Lewis Carroll

'Here is Edward Bear, coming downstairs now, bump, bump, bump, on the back of his head, behind Christopher Robin.'
Winnie-the-Pooh by A. A. Milne

'Mr and Mrs Dursley, of number four, Privet Drive, were proud to say that they were perfectly normal, thank you very much.'
Harry Potter and the Philosopher's Stone by J. K. Rowling

'Lyra and her daemon moved through the darkening Hall, taking care to keep to one side, out of sight of the kitchen.'
Northern Lights by Philip Pullman

UK PAPER SIZES

A0..........841x1189 mm (33.1x46.8 in)	A4...............210x297 mm (8.3x11.7 in)
A1..............594x841 mm (23.4x33.1 in)	A5...............148x210 mm (5.8x8.3 in)
A2..........420x594 mm (16.5x23.4 in)	A6...............105x148 mm (4.1x5.8 in)
A3..............297x420 mm (11.7x16.5 in)	A7...................74x105 mm (2.9x4.1 in)

NON-OLYMPIC GAMES

Beetle herding • Bubble catching • Coin stacking
Competitive blinking • Competitive bumblebee throwing
Deep-sea eating • Endurance laughing • Stunt conkers
Heaviest-schoolbag carrying • Loudest-sneezing

THE FIRST FIVE GS OF ACCELERATION

High acceleration or deceleration subjects you to different experiences of gravity. The faster the rate of change of speed, the higher the 'g-force' and the greater the effect on your body:

1-g The effect of gravity on the surface of the Earth – you feel this all the time.

2-g The force you feel when you take off in an aeroplane. Your arms, legs, hands and feet feel heavy.

3-g The force you feel on a fast roller coaster. You are unable to lift your head to look around and your heart has to work harder to pump blood around your body.

4-g The force you feel in a relatively minor car crash. Your head feels four times heavier, and your neck muscles struggle to cope. Your vision narrows to a small tunnel. Colours fade to white, then to black.

5-g The force felt by fighter pilots when they come out of an extremely fast turn. You may experience gravity-induced loss of consciousness, or g-loc.

WHICH IS A PERFECT CIRCLE?

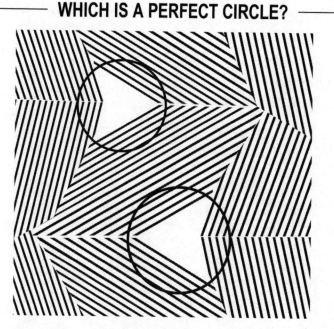

Answer: They both are.

DO YOU SEE IN 3-D?

Hold a finger upright in front of your face, then open and close one eye at a time. Your finger appears to jump to the side. That's because each eye views from a slightly different angle. Your brain blends the images together and there you have it, a 3-D picture.

To test your 3-D vision, hold two pencils horizontally in front of you, level with your eyes. Slowly bring the tips of the two pencils together.

Easy? Now try repeating the exercise with one eye closed.

Closing one eye changes your vision to 2-D, so you can't tell which pencil is in the foreground and which is in the background.

SPIDER BITES

TARANTULA
Swelling, achiness

WHITE-TAILED SPIDER
Blisters, lesions, faintness

FUNNEL-WEB SPIDER
Cramps, rigidity, paralysis

BANANA SPIDER
Immediate pain, cold sweats, possible death

VIOLIN SPIDER
Skin blisters, ulcers, tissue death (necrosis)

SAC SPIDER
Pain two to eight hours after being bitten, swelling, possible scarring

WOLF SPIDER
Pain, itchiness, dizziness, nausea

EXTROVERT — OR — INTROVERT?

Outgoing	Reserved
Easygoing	Complicated
Thinks later	Thinks first
Emotional	Aloof
Changes the world	Understands the world
Breadth	Depth
Action	Ideas
Noise and variety	Quiet and concentration
Lots of people	One-on-one

ORIENTEERING MAP SYMBOLS

Orienteering maps are made for people who want to navigate an area on foot. Features of the landscape are shown in different colours:

Black.....................................Rocks and man-made features

Brown...Landforms

Blue...Water features

Yellow.....................................Easy-to-pass vegetation

Green.....................................Difficult-to-pass vegetation

White.....................................Forest with little or no undergrowth

Purple (or red).....................................The orienteering course

MASS EXTINCTION

Around 249 million years ago, 90 per cent of all marine life and 70 per cent of all land animals were wiped out, including dinosaurs. This mass extinction is thought to have been the result of either an asteroid impact or massive environmental change.

———— AN EASY METHOD ————

You can use the following method (called a 'mnemonic') to remember the order of planets in our solar system: 'My Very Easy Method Just Speeds Up Names'. The first letter of each of the words corresponds with the first letter of one of the planets. Mercury is the planet closest to the Sun, and Neptune is the planet furthest away from the Sun. Pluto is now classified as a dwarf planet.

My..Mercury

Very...Venus

Easy...Earth

Method..Mars

Just..Jupiter

Speeds...Saturn

Up..Uranus

Names..Neptune

———— TEACHER, TEACHER ————

Willy: 'Teacher, teacher, do you think it's right to punish people for things they haven't done?'
Teacher: *'Of course not.'*
Willy: 'Good. I haven't done my homework.'

Teacher: *'You missed school yesterday, didn't you?'*
Willy: 'Not very much, no.'

Teacher: *'Why did you eat your homework, Willy?'*
Willy: 'You told me it was a piece of cake.'

Teacher: *'I wish you would pay a little attention.'*
Willy: 'I can't pay anything. I didn't get my pocket money this week.'

SAILING TERMS

BROACHING
The boat suddenly
tips in the water.

DEATH ROLL
The boat rolls from side
to side until it either capsizes
or the captain takes action.

HEELING
The strength of the wind
makes the boat lean over.

HIKING
The crew lean over
the edge of the boat as it
heels to stop it tipping over.

IN IRONS
The wind blows front-on
and can push the
boat backwards.

JIBING
The boat's stern (rear) is
turned through the wind so
that the wind blows from
the other side.

TACKING
The boat's bow (front) is
turned through the wind
so that the wind blows
from the other side.

DON'T GO ZONE
The wind blows from
directly astern of (behind)
the boat, making it really
difficult to sail.

CAPSIZING
The boat overturns so that
the underside is on top.

CONVERT IT

inches (in) $\xrightarrow{\times 2.54}$ centimetres (cm)
$\times 0.3937$

feet (ft) $\xrightarrow{\times 0.3048}$ metres (m)
$\times 3.2808$

miles (mi) $\xrightarrow{\times 1.6093}$ kilometres (km)
$\times 0.6214$

square inches (sq in) $\xrightarrow{\times 6.4516}$ square centimetres (cm^2)
$\times 0.155$

square feet (sq ft) $\xrightarrow{\times 0.0929}$ square metres (m^2)
$\times 10.7639$

square miles (sq mi) $\xrightarrow{\times 2.59}$ square kilometres (km^2)
$\times 0.3861$

acres $\xrightarrow{\times 0.4047}$ hectares
$\times 2.471$

cubic inches (cu in) $\xrightarrow{\times 16.3871}$ cubic centimetres (cm^3)
$\times 0.0613$

pints $\xrightarrow{\times 56.826}$ centilitres (cl)
$\times 0.0176$

gallons (gal) $\xrightarrow{\times 4.5460}$ litres (l)
$\times 0.22$

ounces (oz) $\xrightarrow{\times 28.3495}$ grams (g)
$\times 0.0353$

pounds (lb) $\xrightarrow{\times 0.454}$ kilograms (kg)
$\times 2.2046$

tons (ton) $\xrightarrow{\times 1016}$ kilograms (kg)
$\times 0.001$

16 ounces in a pound   100 centimetres = 1 metre
12 inches in a foot   1,000 metres = 1 kilometre
2,240 pounds in a ton   1,000 grams = 1 kilogram
8 pints = 1 gallon   100 centilitres = 1 litre

——— TEN WAYS A CRICKET BATSMAN CAN GET OUT ———

1. Bowled

2. Caught

3. Run out

4. Stumped by the wicketkeeper

5. Hitting the ball twice

6. Touching the ball with his hand

7. Hitting his own wicket with his bat

8. LBW (standing in front of the wicket 'leg before wicket')

9. Deliberately obstructing a fielder

10. Timed out (taking longer than three minutes to walk on to the field once the previous player is out)

——— FICTIONAL SCHOOLS ———

Starfleet Academy...*Star Trek*

Springfield Elementary..*The Simpsons*

Bedrock High School...*The Flintstones*

Xavier's School For Gifted Youngsters...............................*X-Men*

Sunnydale High School....................................*Buffy the Vampire Slayer*

Unseen University....................................*The Discworld novels*

Midtown High School......................*Spider-Man's school in the Bronx*

Imperial Academy..*Star Wars*

Pokémon Battle Judge Training Institute...............................Pokémon

Hogwarts School of Witchcraft and Wizardry......................*The Harry Potter novels*

SILLY SUPERHEROES

INEDIBLE MAN
Though he is only the size of a marshmallow and
smells good, he tastes completely disgusting. As soon as
you pop him into your mouth, the gag reflex sends him
shooting across the room to fight another day.

PETER-PIPER-PICKED-A-PECK-OF-PICKLED-PEPPER MAN
'Oh no, it's Peter-Piper-Pecked-a-Pick ... it's Peker-Piker-Kicked
... no, it's Peper-Piper-Peped ... Grrrrrrrrr!' He is neither fast nor
strong, but bad guys lose their demonic enthusiasm when they
stumble on this superhero's awkward name.

SMILE MAN
Smile Man has a disarming smile. When Smile Man
smiles, everybody smiles. Even bad-tempered
villains can't stop grinning.

CAN YOU BUILD IT?

HOW TO MAKE A BALLOON SWORD

1. Blow up a long, thin balloon so that it is not quite full of air. You should be able to easily twist the balloon.

2. Tie a secure knot at the bottom.

3. To make the handle of the sword, twist the balloon about 10 cm (4 in) up from the bottom. Make sure you keep hold of it, so that it doesn't untwist.

4. To form the cross-piece of the sword, make another twist about 8 cm (3 in) up from the first one. Then, make a third twist the same distance from the second one.

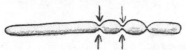

5. Twist the first and last twist together.

6. Twist this with the handle and let go. The first part of the cross-piece is now done and will stay in place.

7. Make two more twists which are again 8 cm (3 in) apart above the first part of the cross-piece.

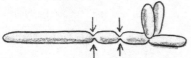

8. Twist the second twist around the first one to make the second part of the cross-piece.

9. Your sword is now complete!

MOON FACTS

- The Moon is 3,476 km (2,160 miles) across.

- The 384,400-km (238,855-mile) journey from Earth to the Moon takes a spaceship about two days. It would take an aeroplane about 26 days.

- The Moon has no brightness of its own. It is lit up by the Sun.

- There are dark spots on the Moon that early astronomers mistook for seas and lakes. In fact they are dry surface features, but have kept their watery names and are called things like 'The Sea of Tranquillity' and 'The Lake of Sorrow'.

SPOONERISMS

Spoonerisms are phrases where the first letters or sounds of words get mixed up through a slip of the tongue.

Pouring with rain...Roaring with pain

Block of flats...Flock of bats

Keen as mustard..Mean as custard

Lighting a fire...Fighting a liar

A half-formed wish.......................................A half-warmed fish

I hit my funny bone......................................I hit my bunny phone

HOOF HEARTED, ICE MELTED

Say this quickly:

'One smart man, he felt smart. Two smart men, they felt smart. Three smart men, they all felt smart.'

THE HISTORY OF SKATEBOARDING

1950 Bored surfers invent a device called a 'truck' that holds wheels to a board and allows a skater to steer the board by shifting his or her weight around.

1958 The first skateboards go on sale in a small surf shop in California, USA.

1963 The first skate contest takes place at a school in Hermosa, California.

1965 Skateboarding booms, becomes mainstream, loses its cool, then dies out.

1970 The invention of 'kick tail' boards and polyurethane wheels with bearings dramatically increase the manoeuvrability of skateboards, and the sport becomes popular again.

1978 Alan 'Ollie' Gelfand performs the first 'ollie', a skateboarding jump that almost all modern-day tricks are based on. Skaters can now jump over objects.

1981 The first edition of Thrasher magazine, a guide for underground skaters, is published.

1985 Vert riding (skating on ramps and other vertical structures) and street-style skating become popular. Professional skaters start competing for big money.

1987 'New school' skating, with an emphasis on technical tricks, becomes popular.

1995 ESPN host the first ever X Games, bringing lots of mainstream attention to the sport.

2003 The first Go Skateboarding Day is held on June 21st.

WAYS TO BREAK A WEREWOLF CURSE

Remove your animal-skin belt, in case it is enchanted.

Kneel in one spot for a hundred years.

Be saluted with the sign of the cross.

Be addressed three times by your baptismal name.

Be struck three times on the forehead with a knife, drawing at least three drops of blood.

Get someone to throw an iron object at you.

HOW TO MAKE A BIRD FEEDER

You will need crushed peanuts, sunflower seeds, oats, raisins, mild grated cheese, water, a large, open pine cone and a length of string.

1. Mix the peanuts, sunflower seeds, oats, raisins and cheese in a bowl.

2. Add a little water to your mixture to make it sticky.

3. Push the mixture into the gaps in the pine cone.

4. Tie a piece of string around the stuffed pine cone and hang it in your garden, ideally somewhere you can see it from a window.

5. It may take a while for the birds to pluck up the courage to visit your feeder, but be patient – they will do.

DONKEY OR SEAL?

STRANGE THINGS SOLD ON THE INTERNET

Second-hand false teeth • Half-eaten chocolate bar

A celebrity's chewed chewing gum • Toenail clippings

An empty cardboard box • A bottle of air

A crisp packet • A person's hand in marriage

GROSS FOOD RECORDS

LARGEST CUSTARD-PIE FIGHT
The world's largest custard-pie fight was fought in Bolton, England, on 29 August 2005. A total of 3,320 pies were thrown by two teams of ten people in three minutes.

FASTEST KETCHUP DRINKING
On 17 February 2012, Benedikt Weber of Germany drank a standard 396 g (13.9 oz) glass bottle of tomato ketchup through a drinking straw in 32.37 seconds.

MOST SAUSAGES EATEN IN ONE MINUTE
On 22 July 2001, Stefan Paladin of New Zealand ate eight whole sausages in one minute. Each sausage measured 10 cm (3.93 in) in length and 2 cm (0.79 in) in width.

MOST ICE CREAM EATEN IN 30 SECONDS
America's Patrick Bertoletti holds the record for eating the most ice cream in 30 seconds using a teaspoon. He consumed 382 g (13.5 oz) of vanilla ice cream in 30 seconds on 7 September 2006.

MOST BRUSSELS SPROUTS EATEN IN ONE MINUTE
Linus Urbanec of Sweden managed to eat 31 Brussels sprouts in one minute on 26 November 2008.

LONGEST PANCAKE MARATHON
On 24 October 1999, Mike Cuzzacrea flipped a pancake continually in a frying pan for just over three hours as he ran the 26.2-mile (40-km) New York Marathon.

─── ARE YOU A BORN CRIMINAL? ───

According to the theories of the 19th-century criminologist Cesare Lombroso, there are 18 key physical indicators of the born criminal:

1. An unusually short or tall body
2. Long arms
3. Sloping shoulders, but large chest
4. Pointy or stubbed fingers or toes
5. Wrinkles on forehead and face
6. Beaked or flat nose
7. Large, protruding ears
8. Strong jawline
9. High cheekbones
10. Oversized incisors
11. Small or weak chin
12. Receding hairline
13. Small head, but large face
14. Small and sloping forehead
15. Fleshy lips or thin upper lip
16. Large eye sockets, but deep-set eyes
17. Bumps on back of head and around ear
18. Bushy eyebrows, tending to meet across nose

─── SMALL ───	─── LARGE ───
Petite • Mini	Massive • Big
Little • Teeny	Gargantuan • Giant
Tiny • Minuscule	Colossal • Huge
Diminutive • Wee	Enormous • Giant
Minute • Miniature	Gigantic • Monster
Microscopic • Baby	Vast • Whopping

ARE THESE LINES HORIZONTAL?

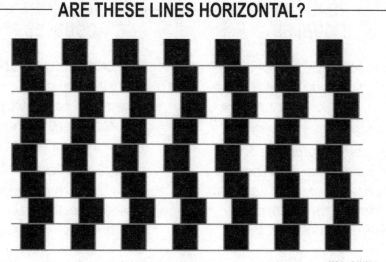

Answer: Yes!

SECRET SOCIETY OATH

'I promise never to reveal the existence of the society to anyone else without first swearing them to the secret oath. I promise never to speak of the business of the society or to trade secrets with another society for personal gain. I promise never to reveal secret hiding places or code names. I swear this on all that is best kept secret.'

CITIES WITH THE MOST UNDERGROUND RAILWAY LINES

New York, USA...24

Paris, France..16

Madrid, Spain...13

London, England..12

Mexico City, Mexico..12

Moscow, Russia..12

Seoul, South Korea...12

Berlin, Germany..10

Tokyo, Japan..9

Barcelona, Spain..8

REAL-LIFE DOUBLES

IMPERSONATOR
A person who mimics your voice and/or mannerisms.

POLITICAL DECOY
A person employed to impersonate a politician in order to draw attention away from them or to take risks on their behalf.

BODY DOUBLE
Someone who substitutes for an actor in dangerous or sexually explicit scenes.

LOOKALIKE
A living person who closely resembles another person, often a celebrity, politician, or member of royalty.

FOLKLORE DOUBLES

DOPPELGÄNGER
A spirit who looks exactly like you, but casts no shadow and has no reflection in a mirror or water.

SHADOWMAN
A black, human-like silhouette that lacks a mouth or eyes. It appears on the edge of your field of vision and disintegrates when noticed.

EVIL TWIN
Exists in another dimension but occasionally enters your world through a porthole. If you catch sight of it you are in danger.

The eyes of a giant squid can be up to 40 cm (15 in) wide.

MADE INTO MUSICALS

The sinking of RMS *Titanic*..*Titanic*

British Prime Minister Margaret Thatcher.............*Thatcher: The Musical*

TV programme *Jerry Springer*.........................*Jerry Springer: The Opera*

International cherry pit-spitting competition..................*Spittin' Distance*

The electric chair...*Fields of Ambrosia*

SUN FACTS

The Sun is the star at the centre of our solar system.

It is a huge ball of hydrogen and helium gas.

Earth is 150 million km (93 million miles) from the Sun.

You could fit over a million Earths into the Sun.

All the planets of our solar system, including Earth,
orbit the Sun.

The Sun is approximately 400 times wider than Earth's Moon.
The reason they appear to be about the same size is because
the Sun is 400 times further away from us.

The temperature at the Sun's core is about
16,600,000°C (28,100,000°F).

The Sun's heat and light support almost all life on Earth.

The Sun's lifetime is predicted to be around 10 billion years.
At the moment it is about 4.5 billion years old.

UNCOMMON CITRUS FRUITS

Ugli fruit • Buddha's hand • Dekopon

Rough lemon • Bitter orange • Kumquat

Limequat • Pomelo • Ponkan • Limetta • Natsumikan

HOW TO WRITE A LIMERICK

A limerick is a poem with a very specific structure. Limericks traditionally start with 'There once was a ...' and are made up of five lines. The first, second and fifth lines have eight syllables and the last syllables of each one should rhyme. The third and fourth lines have five syllables and a different rhyme.

1. Think of a character you would like to write about and give them a name. Now write an eight-syllable sentence ending with that name. For example:
    There once was a lion called Len,

2. Think of as many words as you can that rhyme with the name you have chosen. Select one to go at the end of the second eight-syllable line, so that the story is continued. For example:
    Who lived in a quiet, cosy den.

3. Now write the next two lines. Remember that these are made up of five syllables and should have a different rhyme. For example:
    He liked to stay in,
    And open a tin,

4. Now finish off your limerick. The last line is another eight-syllable line. It should rhyme with the first two lines and finish off your story. For example:
    And never went hunting again.

ANIMALS IN ORDER OF INTELLIGENCE

1. Human	8. Whale
2. Chimpanzee	9. Dolphin
3. Gorilla	10. Elephant
4. Orang-utan	11. Pig
5. Baboon	12. Dog
6. Gibbon	13. Cat
7. Monkey	14. Octopus

THE DREADED KRAKEN

Sailors beware the fabled sea monster known as the Kraken. The monster's immense, rounded back resembles an island. Desperate for dry land, sea-weary sailors have been known to drop anchor and row out to it. Before settling down for a night's rest, the fires are lit – at which point the Kraken wakes up. The unfortunate sailors are drowned. Or worse.

APPLE-PIP FORTUNES

Cut an apple in half. The number of seeds you see will tell you your fortune.

One seed.......................................Good luck

Two seeds......................................Marriage

Three seeds....................................Wealth

Four seeds.....................................Travel

Five seeds.....................................Health

Six seeds......................................Wisdom

Seven seeds....................................Fame

TRACE THE SHAPES

Shapes that can be traced in one continuous line, without taking your pencil off the page and without tracing along any line twice:

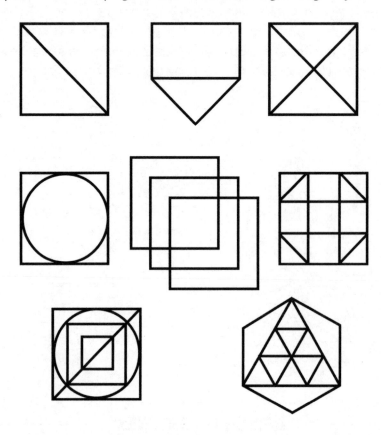

A GRUESOME EXECUTION

In 1757, the execution of Robert-François Damiens, who attempted to assassinate the French King Louis XV, began with torture using red-hot pincers. The hand with which he'd held a knife was then burnt off using sulphur. Next, molten wax, lead and boiling oil were poured into his wounds. Horses were then harnessed to his arms and legs and made to run in opposite directions so that his limbs would rip off. But his joints wouldn't tear, so the executioner had to cut through them with a knife. Even after all this agonizing torture, Damiens was rumoured not to have died, and his head and torso were later burnt at the stake.

THE POLES

The North and South Poles are the points at which the Earth's axis of rotation meets the surface of the Earth.

THE NORTH POLE

The exact North Pole, called the Geographic North Pole, is located in the Arctic Ocean. In whichever direction you travel from the Geographic North Pole, you are always heading south.

Magnetic North is the place to which all magnetic compasses point. It is not the same point as the Geographic North Pole.

The North Pole has 24 hours of daylight during the summer months and 24 hours of darkness during the winter months.

THE SOUTH POLE

The exact South Pole, called the Geographic South Pole, is located in the continent of Antarctica. In whichever direction you travel from the Geographic South Pole, you are always heading north.

The Ceremonial South Pole is an area set aside for photo opportunities a few hundred metres from the Geographic South Pole.

The ice cap at the South Pole is 3,000 m (9,840 ft) thick, but the ice is melting. Over 13,000 square km (8,000 square miles) of sea ice has been lost in Antarctica over the last 50 years. This is generally thought to be the consequence of global warming.

SURF SPEAK

Dawn patrol..Getting up early for a morning surf

Regular footer.............................Surfer who rides left foot forwards

Goofy footer.............................Surfer who rides right foot forwards

Kook...Hopeless surfer

Dude..Everyone and anyone

Beach breaks..Constant waves

Point breaks...Perfect waves

Gnarly.....................The sea when the waves are very choppy

Shredding...Surfing like a pro

Aerial.....................Jumping your board into the air above a wave

Wicked drop in...........................Stealing another person's wave

Insane...Anything that's cool

Stoked...Really happy

Surfed out...In need of a rest

TOO MUCH TV

Goggle eyes • TV addict • Square eyes • Couch potato
Sofa sloth • Technicolour dreamer

CURSED

THE CURSE OF THE PHARAOHS

There is a belief that any person who disturbs the tomb of an ancient Egyptian pharaoh will die shortly afterwards. The curse struck the team who opened the tomb of Pharaoh Tutankhamen in 1922. Within six years of the tomb's discovery, 12 of the archaeologists were dead, including the expedition's patron, Lord Carnarvon, who died 47 days after entering the tomb.

THE HOPE DIAMOND

Part of the French crown jewels worn by Marie Antoinette at her execution, the diamond is thought to bring bad luck to whomever possesses it. Owners have met their deaths as a result of suicides, car crashes and cliff falls.

ANCIENT ROMAN CURSES

The ancient Romans had a formula for making an enemy suffer an injury. They wrote curses on lead tablets, known as 'tabulae defixiones' and put them in a tomb or a sacred spring.

TECUMSEH'S CURSE

Between 1840 and 1960, all the US presidents elected in the years divisible by 20 died in office. This is said to stem from a curse issued by the Indian chief Tecumseh in 1811, when General William Henry Harrison defeated Tecumseh in battle and won the presidency. Harrison caught a cold soon after and died, having spent just one month in office. The curse was broken by Ronald Reagan, elected in 1980, who survived an assassin's bullet by less than an inch.

SCAMMER'S LANGUAGE

Con or scam..............An attempt to trick someone out of something

Grifter...The con artist

Mark or pigeon..The victim

Shill.............................A grifter's accomplice who pretends to be a member of the public as part of the scam

HOW TO MAKE A WATER CLOCK

Here is a simple method of making a time-keeping device, an essential skill if you are forced to survive in the middle of nowhere.

1. Cut the top off a plastic two-litre bottle, about 8 cm (3 in) from the top.

2. Stick a strip of masking tape on the outside of the bottle, so that it runs in a straight line from the top to the bottom.

3. Make a small hole in the bottom of a paper cup and fit the cup snugly into the opening you cut at the top of the bottle.

4. Have a stopwatch ready in front of you. Fill the cup with water. The moment you start pouring, start the stopwatch.

5. Every minute, mark the water level on the masking tape. Always make sure the paper cup is at least half full with water, so that it runs into the bottle in a steady stream.

6. Once the bottle is filled with water and you've made all the markings, you can use the 'clock' to keep track of the time.

REAL PARTS OF A SWISS ARMY KNIFE

Large blade
Small blade
Corkscrew
Can opener
Small screwdriver
Bottle opener
Pliers
Tweezers
Torch
Scissors

PARTS OF A SWISS ARMY KNIFE NOT YET INVENTED

Skeleton key
Grappling hook
Pea-shooter
Industrial laser
Bugging device
Miniature fishing reel
Universal remote control
Digital voice recorder
Invisible-ink pen
Telescope

SYMMETRICAL WORDS

If you were to draw a horizontal line through the middle of the following words, the top of the word would be a mirror image of the bottom:

COOKBOOK	BIKED
EXCEEDED	DICED
HOODED	CHOKE
DEED	CHOICE
BEDECKED	HIKED
CHEEK	BOBBED

THE OLDEST EVER

Mollusc	507 years old
Giant tortoise	183 years old
Human	122 years old
Elephant	86 years old
Cat	38 years old
Leopard	23 years old
Pig	22 years old

It takes just $\frac{1}{50}$ of a second for the guillotine blade to sever the head from the neck, though it has been suggested that it may take up to seven seconds for the brain to lose consciousness after the head is severed.

IS THIS ART?

Some important modern artworks have included:

- A urinal
- A pile of bricks
- An unmade bed
- A rubbish bin
- A black canvas
- A sheep cut in half
- A wrapped-up dog kennel
- An empty room with a light bulb that repeatedly goes on and off.

HOW TO MAKE A COMPASS

You will need a clear glass bowl filled with water, a 0.5-cm (0.2-in) slice from the end of a cork, a magnet and a needle.

1. Float the cork in the bowl of water.
2. Magnetize the needle by rubbing it over the magnet in the same direction about fifty times.
3. Lay the needle on the cork.

The needle will slowly turn to line up with the Earth's North and South Magnetic Poles.

LOUDEST EVER HUMAN NOISES

Burp..............................109.9 decibels, Paul Hunn, UK, 23 August 2009

Whistle........................125 decibels, Marco Ferrera, USA, 7 July 2004

Knuckle crack............83.2 decibels, Miguel Ángel Molano, Spain, 25 May 2012

HOW TO CHART YOUR FAMILY TREE

1. Write your name at the bottom of a large piece of paper.

2. If you have any brothers or sisters, write their names alongside yours, oldest on the left, youngest on the right.

3. Draw a vertical line out of the top of each of the names. Finish each line at the same point, then join the top of the lines together with a horizontal line.

4. Draw a vertical line upwards from the centre of the horizontal line.

5. Starting at the top of the vertical line, draw a short horizontal line to either side.

6. Write your father's name on the left of the line and your mother's name on the right. Your family tree should now look something like this:

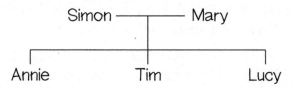

7. Write the names of your father's brothers and sisters to the left of his name, and your mother's brothers and sisters to the right of her name, in age order from left to right.

8. Connect the names of the brothers and sisters in your father's family, and draw a vertical line to the names of their parents (your grandparents) in the same way you connected the names of the children in your family to your parents. Now do the same for your mother's side of the family.

9. Write the names of your grandparents' brothers and sisters next to your grandparents' names, and connect them to the names of their parents (your great-grandparents).

10. Continue this pattern to trace your family tree back as far as you can - ask your relatives to help you find out all the names. You may also wish to add everyone's date of birth.

HOMEMADE INSTRUMENTS

DRUMS
Stretch different materials (such as carrier bags or balloons)
tightly over pots of different sizes using elastic bands to secure
them and strike with a salad spoon.

MARACAS
Fill a plastic water bottle or tea caddy
with rice, pebbles, coffee beans, or sand. Vitamin-tablet
pots are ready-made maracas.

CYMBALS
Bang two saucepan lids together.

XYLOPHONES
Fill drinking glasses or glass bottles with varying amounts
of water and line them up from most to least full. Tap
each glass with a pencil to produce different notes.

The ancient Greek mathematician Hero invented
the vending machine in Alexandria. The coin
dropped on to a lever which opened a valve
and out flowed a small amount of holy water.

TIPS FOR AVOIDING BEE STINGS

1. Never try to swat a honeybee. Bees are generally passive unless annoyed or threatened, and usually only sting in self-defence.

2. Smell horrible. Bees like flowers that smell nice. You stink, they fly away.

3. Wear camouflage. Bees have poor eyesight and won't be able to spot you wearing light colours in the day and dark colours at night.

4. Never mow the lawn. The low buzzing of motorized garden tools can agitate swarms, hives or colonies.

5. Keep your shoes on. Particularly avoid walking barefoot over lawns that contain blooming clover, which bees love.

6. If a bee head-butts you, move quickly in the opposite direction. Sentry bees patrolling the edges of the hive's territory do this to warn off invaders.

7. Stay indoors until sunset. Bees generally sleep after dark.

THE SPEED YOU MAKE THE AIR MOVE

Inhaling	6 kph (4 mph)
Sniffing	30 kph (20 mph)
Coughing	100 kph (60 mph)
Sneezing	160 kph (100 mph)

RETIRED HURRICANE NAMES

All hurricanes are given a name from a long list. If an unusually destructive hurricane hits, its name is retired and never used again. Among those retired are:

Allison • Floyd • Georges • Keith

Iris • Lenny • Michelle

SPONTANEOUS HUMAN COMBUSTION

Throughout history, there have been many documented cases of people going up in flames for no apparent reason. The following evidence makes it look as though the flames that devoured the victims came from inside their own bodies:

Despite its severity, the fire is confined to the body. Clothing is barely singed, and flammable objects nearby remain untouched.

Portions of the body, such as an arm or a foot, remain unburned.

The torso usually suffers severe burning and in some cases is reduced to ash.

A greasy soot deposit covers the ceiling and walls.

Suggested but unconvincing theories for spontaneous human combustion include:

Static electricity build-up

Flammable body fat

The short-circuiting of the body's electrical fields

An explosive combination of digestive chemicals

High levels of alcohol in the body

THE LONGEST-EVER HAIRS

Mohican....1.14 m (3.74 ft), Kazuhiro Watanabe, Japan, October 2011

Eyebrow.........18.1 cm (7.1 in), Sumito Matsumura, Japan, 30 June 2011

Leg hair..................19.01 cm (7.48 in), Guido Arturo, Italy, 31 March 2012

Ear hair.............18.1 cm (7.12 in), Anthony Victor, India, 26 August 2007

STICK PUZZLE

Take away nine sticks to form only four squares.
All squares (large and small) are counted and each
stick must be part of a square.

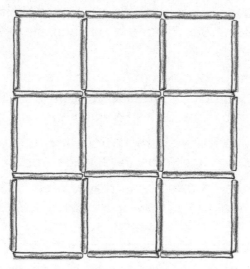

Answer on page 230

HOW TO PLAY 'CUPS'

1. This is a game to be played in a swimming pool, lake or the sea. Two players stand back-to-back in waist-deep water.

2. Choose one player to be the cupper and one person to be the guesser.

3. At the count of three, both players must duck underwater. The cupper then swims one stroke either to the left or to the right. At the same time, the guesser swims one stroke in the direction that they think the cupper will have swum.

4. If, when both players resurface, they are in the same place, the guesser has guessed correctly and takes the point. If they are two strokes apart, the cupper has outsmarted the guesser and the cupper takes the point.

5. After three games, the player with the most wins takes the role of the cupper.

THE OFFSIDE RULE IN FOOTBALL

The offside rule is said to be football's most complicated rule. Understanding the rule traditionally distinguishes real football fans from everyone else.

An attacking player is in an offside position if he is nearer his opponents' goal line than both the ball and the last defender (not including the goalie).

However, the player is only penalized for being in an offside position if his team gain an advantage from it at the moment the ball is played by one of his teammates.

When defenders deliberately move forwards to try to put an attacker offside, it is known as the 'offside trap'.

There is no offence if the offside player receives the ball directly from a goal kick, throw-in or corner kick.

If you get stuck in the middle of your spaceship in zero gravity and are unable to reach the floor, ceiling or walls, do not despair. Instead, take off a shoe and throw it across the cabin. You and your shoe will act as a pair of equal and opposite forces, propelling you backwards. The harder you throw your shoe, the faster you will be pushed away from it.

EMBARRASSED AT SCHOOL

Your mum kisses you goodbye at the school gate.

Your sister follows you, calling you by your family nickname.

You get chosen last when picking teams for P.E.

Your parents make friends with the parents of the school geek, and they arrange for you all to go on holiday together.

There's a stink in the toilets. Everyone's talking about it, and you're responsible.

FAMOUS LAST WORDS

THE SCIENTIST
The 19th-century British surgeon Joseph Henry Green checked his own pulse, announced 'Stopped', and then died.

THE POET
The German poet Heinrich Heine never got to give his last message to the world, his final words being 'Write ... write ... pencil ... paper.'

THE PLAYWRIGHT
The Norwegian dramatist Henrik Ibsen heard his nurse tell a visitor that he was feeling better. 'On the contrary,' Ibsen said, and died.

THE ACTOR
Hollywood swashbuckler Douglas Fairbanks declared 'I've never felt better', and promptly died.

THE PHILOSOPHER
The German political philosopher Karl Marx was asked by his maid if he had any last words. He replied, 'Go on, get out! Last words are for fools who haven't said enough!'

THE WIT
The last words of Oscar Wilde are believed to be: 'Either this wallpaper goes or I do.'

You can't stop yourself vomiting by keeping your mouth shut. The sick will just come out of your nose instead.

HOW NOT TO GET EATEN BY A POLAR BEAR

1. Bears hate noise. So, if you see one nearby, shout and scream out as loud as you can to keep it at bay.

2. If a polar bear approaches you, always act in a non-threatening manner. Lower your eyes to the ground, avoiding eye-contact, and back slowly away.

3. If the bear continues to approach, stand your ground, hold your arms over your head (or better still your coat) to make yourself look bigger, and make more noise.

FAKE HARRY POTTER BOOKS IN CHINA

Harry Potter and the Porcelain Doll

Harry Potter and the Leopard-Walk-Up-To-Dragon

Harry Potter and the Golden Turtle

Harry Potter and the Crystal Vase

What do astronauts drink?

Gravi-tea

CLOTHING SIZES AROUND THE WORLD

WOMEN'S CLOTHES

American	4	6	8	10	12	14
British	8	10	12	14	16	18
Continental	36	38	40	42	44	46

MEN'S CLOTHES

American	34	36	38	40	42	44
British	34	36	38	40	42	44
Continental	44	46	48	50	52	54

CHILDREN'S CLOTHES

American	4	6	8	10	12	14
British						
Height (cm)	110	120	130	140	150	160
Age	4-5	6-8	9-10	11	12	13
Continental						
Height (cm)	125	135	150	155	160	165
Age	7	9	12	13	14	15

Army ants of South America don't have nests. They live on the move, foraging as they go. Anything in their path, including animals, is likely to be eaten alive.

A LIGHT-BULB PROBLEM

You are in a room with three light switches labelled 1, 2, 3. One of the light switches controls a bulb you can't see that is in the next room. All three switches are off and the light bulb is off. You can flick any of the switches as many times as you want, for as long as you want. You can then go into the next room once to check the bulb. How will you find out which switch is connected to the bulb?

Turn switch 1 on for 10 minutes, then turn it off. Turn switch 2 on then immediately go to check the bulb. If it is off and hot it is switch 1. If it is on it is switch 2. If it is off and cold it is switch 3.

—— CHRISTMAS DINNERS AROUND THE WORLD ——

Turkey...Salted dry cod with boiled potatoes

Romania...Stuffed cabbage

Russia..Meat dumplings

Sweden................Baked ham, pickled herring, lutfish and rice pudding

Poland...............................Beetroot soup, prune dumplings, carp

Britain..Roasted goose

Germany...Carp or goose

USA..Roasted turkey

—— ONE YEAR IN SPACE ——

A year is the amount of time it takes
for a planet to go around the Sun.

PLANET	DISTANCE FROM SUN (million miles)	LENGTH OF YEAR (in Earth days)
Mercury	36	88
Venus	67	225
Earth	93	365
Mars	142	687
Jupiter	484	4,333
Saturn	887	10,750
Uranus	1,784	30,707
Neptune	2,796	60,202

The one-syllable word 'are' can be changed
into a three-syllable word by adding the
single letter 'a' to the end of it.

REALLY LONG WALKS

THE MEDIEVAL PILGRIMAGE
Medieval pilgrims walked 1,600 km (1,000 miles) from France to reach the holy shrine in Santiago de Compostela, Spain.

THE APPALACHIAN TRAIL
This 3,487-km (2,167-mile) trail through the Appalachian Mountains of America is the longest hiking trail in the world.

THE SILK ROAD
In 100 BC Chinese silk merchants travelled 6,000 km (3,700 miles) along the Silk Road from China to Imperial Rome.

THE GREAT WALL OF CHINA
Also known as 'the longest graveyard on Earth', this ancient fortification stretches 2,400 km (1,500 miles) through scorching deserts, mountains and dangerous forests.

HOW WATERY?

A tomato	95%
A potato	80%
A human	75%
A loaf of bread	35%

THE FORMING OF THE CONTINENTS

By looking at the structure of the Earth, it is possible to form theories about how the continents we have today came into being.

YEARS AGO	CONTINENTS
3 billion	There was one continent called Ur *which split into*
2.5 billion	Ur and Arctica *which split into*
2 billion	Ur, Arctica, Baltica and Atlantica *then Arctica and Baltica joined to form Nena, so the continents were*
1.5 billion	Nena, Ur and Atlantica *then Nena, Ur and Atlantica joined to form*
1 billion	Rodinia *which split into*
700 million	Nena, Atlantica and Ur *which joined again to form*
300 million	Pangaea *which eventually split into*
200 million	Africa, Antarctica, Australia, Europe, Asia, North America and South America

GREETINGS IN DIFFERENT COUNTRIES

Japan....................Bow from the waist, palms on thighs, heels together

France...A kiss on both cheeks

New Zealand Maoris...A touching of noses

Britain..A handshake

India...With palms pressed together as though praying, a bend or nod

MAJOR RISKS OF SPACE TRAVEL

Becoming separated from the ship during a space-walk
Blacking out during take-off
Crash-landing on an airless planet
Being hit by a meteor
Being exposed to radiation
Burning up on re-entering the Earth's atmosphere

EINSTEIN'S PUZZLE

Three dragons, Dudley, Delilah and Dave, live in three separate holes, numbered 1, 2, 3 from left to right. They each have a favourite rock band (The Scaly Singers, The Winged Wonders and The Fire Breathers) and a favourite ice-cream flavour (vanilla, strawberry and chocolate). Based on the following information, which dragon loves chocolate ice cream and which dragon listens to The Scaly Singers?

Dudley loves vanilla ice cream.

Delilah's favourite rock band is The Fire Breathers.

The dragon that lives in the left hole is a fan of
The Winged Wonders.

Dudley and Delilah have one hole separating them.

The Scaly Singers fan does not live on the left of
the strawberry ice-cream lover.

Answer: Delilah loves chocolate ice cream. Dave listens to The Scaly Singers

HAND SHADOWS

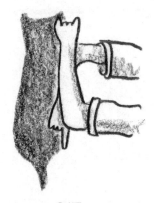

CAT

DOG

SNAIL

BIRD

GALILEO'S SHIP

You are in a cabin below the deck of a ship. You have with you: two goldfish in a bowl, a ball and a stick of incense. When the boat is at anchor, the goldfish swim with equal effort in all directions, the ball falls straight down from your hands to the floor, and the incense smoke drifts directly upwards into the air. When the boat is moving in a straight line and at an even pace, will these effects change?

Answer: No. Everything contained in the ship, including the air, is moving at the same rate.

HIGH DIVING

BACKWARD
The diver takes off with his
or her back to the water.

PIKE
The body is folded in half,
bent at the waist but
not at the knees.

LAYOUT
The body is
completely straight.

TUCK
The body is curled into
a ball, with the knees
brought up to the chin and
the heels tucked against
the back of the legs.

WATER ENTRANCE
The diver must be
straight, powerful and
make a minimal splash.

The world's highest ever dive, a double-back somersault
from 54 m (177 ft), was performed by the Swiss diver
Olivi er Favre in Villers-le-Lac, France, in 1987.

In 1998, the Swiss diver Frederic Weill performed a dive
from a helicopter into Lake Verbano in Italy. The 26 m (86 ft)
dive included an armstand take-off and double somersault pike.

The highest ever shallow dive was performed by Darren Taylor
from Colorado, USA, on 17 March 2011. He dived from a height
of 11 m (36 ft) into 30.5 cm (12 in) of water.

Camels' humps do not contain water as is commonly
believed, but instead store fatty tissue for when
food is scarce. The fat supply is enough for them
to survive without a drink for about two weeks, and
without food for up to a month.

EGYPTIAN HIEROGLYPHS

Ancient Egyptians wrote using hieroglyphics – a script made up of pictures. There are few clues as to how Egyptians pronounced their words, but here are some hieroglyphs that roughly translate to the letters of our alphabet (there is no equivalent for 'x').

a	b	c	d	e
as in 'ant'	as in 'bat'	as in 'loch'	as in 'dad'	as in 'eat'

f	g	h	i	j
as in 'fog'	as in 'got'	as in 'hat'	as in 'pin'	as in 'jump'

k	l	m	n	o
as in 'kite'	as in 'lot'	as in 'mum'	as in 'not'	as in 'who'

p	q	r	s	t
as in 'pin'	as in 'quit'	as in 'run'	as in 'sit'	as in 'top'

u	v	w	y	z
as in 'glue'	as in 'van'	as in 'wig'	as in 'baby'	as in 'zoo'

WHAT KIND OF -PHILE ARE YOU?

'-phile' is the opposite of '-phobe' and means 'loving'.

Turophile..Cheese

Hippophile..Horses

Ophiophile..Snakes

Nyctophile...Darkness

Hoplophile..Weaponry

Xylophile...Wood

Logophile...Words

Technophile..Technology

Claustrophile...................................Enclosed spaces

Thalassophile..Seas

Francophile..France

Bibliophile...Books

TYPES OF FIREWORK

Star shells • Mini mines • Mini bombettes • Salutes • Jacks
Cones • Helicopters • Planes • UFOs • Snakes • Racers
Bottle rockets • Catherine wheels • Bangers

———————— WHAT'S THE DIFFERENCE? ————————

INDIAN AND AFRICAN ELEPHANTS
The African elephant is larger than the Indian elephant and has larger ears. The African elephant has two lips on its trunk, while the Indian elephant only has one.

STALAGMITES AND STALACTITES
These icicle-shaped pillars form over thousands of years where water drips through the roof of a limestone cave, leaving mineral deposits behind. Stalagmites grow up from the ground while stalactites grow down from the roof of the cave.

INTERNET AND THE WORLD WIDE WEB
The Internet is a massive network in which any computer can communicate with any other computer as long as they are both connected to the Internet. The World Wide Web is just one way of accessing information on the Internet. It uses a computer-programming language called HTTP. This is just one of the many languages used over the Internet.

COCA-COLA AND PEPSI-COLA
Coca-Cola was invented in 1886, followed by Pepsi in 1898. It is assumed that Coca-Cola was named after the coca leaves and kola nuts used to make it. Pepsi was named after the beneficial effects it was believed to have on a kind of bellyache called dyspepsia.

———————— MONOPOLY RECORDS ————————

Longest anti-gravitational game (played on the ceiling)........36 hours

Longest game played in a bath..99 hours

Longest game played in a lift...16 days

Longest game played underwater..50 days

Longest game ever played...70 days

A KNOT TRICK

This is a handy trick to have up your sleeve if you want to win a bet. Tell your friends to try and tie a knot in a piece of string without letting go of the ends. They won't be able to do it. Follow this guide to show them how it's done.

With a piece of string on a table in front of you, cross your arms, as shown. One hand should be on top of the opposite arm and the other hand tucked under the opposite armpit.

Holding this position, lean forward and pick up one end and then the other, so you have an end of the string in each hand.

Now simply uncross your arms.

You'll be left with a neat knot in the centre of the string.

> Ostriches can run at 72 kph (45 mph) for nearly 20 minutes at a time.

BALLET TERMS

GLISSADE
Gliding
PIROUETTE
Complete turn on one leg
ARABESQUE
Standing on one leg,
leaning forward, with the
other leg stretched back
ENTRECHAT
Crossing and uncrossing
of feet during a jump
JETÉ
Jumping from one foot
to the other
POINTE
Dancing on tiptoes

PLIÉ
Bending knees

Moths are not attracted to light. They
fly towards the blackest point which
appears to be behind the light.

THE LARGEST COUNTRIES

Russia.............................17,075,200 square km (6,592,735 square miles)

Canada..........................9,976,140 square km (3,851,788 square miles)

China.............................9,596,960 square km (3,705,386 square miles)

USA................................9,372,610 square km (3,618,764 square miles)

Brazil.............................8,511,965 square km (3,286,470 square miles)

Australia........................7,686,850 square km (2,967,893 square miles)

WORLD STANDARDS

METRE
A metre was originally a French standard of measurement. It was said to be one ten-millionth part of the distance from the North Pole to the equator, when measured on a straight line running along the surface of the Earth through Paris. Today, a metre is the distance travelled by light in a vacuum during 1/299,792,458 of a second.

FATHOM
Sailors used to measure the depth of water using a long, weighted rope called a sounding line. A fathom was the length of rope that a man could hold between his extended arms as he hauled it out of the sea. One fathom is 1.8 m (6 ft) long. In old English the word 'fathom' means 'outstretched arm'.

MILE
Roman soldiers kept track of the distances they marched by counting their paces. One pace was a double step. One mile was a thousand paces - in Latin, *mille passas*.

What is a robot's favourite part of the school day?

Assembly

LIZARD NAMES

Alectrosaurus	Unmarried lizard
Deinodon	Terrible tooth
Gasosaurus	Gas lizard
Nanosaurus	Dwarf lizard
Quaesitosaurus	Abnormal lizard
Saichania	Beautiful one
Ultrasaurus	Ultra giant lizard
Xenotarsosaurus	Strange-ankle lizard

A WITCH'S SPELL

Double, double toil and trouble;
Fire burn, and cauldron bubble.
...

Fillet of a fenny snake,
In the cauldron boil and bake;
Eye of newt and toe of frog,
Wool of bat and tongue of dog,
Adder's fork and blind-worm's sting;
Lizard's leg and howlet's wing,
For a charm of powerful trouble,
Like a hell-broth boil and bubble.
...

Double, double toil and trouble;
Fire burn, and cauldron bubble.
...

Cool it with a baboon's blood,
Then the charm is firm and good.

A camel-hair brush is made of squirrel fur.

TEXTOGRAMS

Textograms are words formed from the same number
sequence on a telephone keypad. They are often
mixed up when texting.

269..boy, box, cow

4663..home, good, gone, hood, hoof

328..fat, eat

7664..snog, song

2253..bake, cake, bald, calf

5693..love, loud

RIVERS FROM SOURCE TO SEA

THE NILE
Source: Lake Victoria, east-central Africa
Sea: Mediterranean Sea
Journey: 6,695 km (4,160 miles)

THE GANGES
Source: Himalayan Mountains, India
Sea: Indian Ocean
Journey: 2,510 km (1,560 miles)

THE AMAZON
Source: Andes Mountains, Peru
Sea: Atlantic Ocean
Journey: 6,275 km (3,899 miles)

THE RHINE
Source: Swiss Alps, Switzerland
Sea: North Sea
Journey: 1,320 km (820 miles)

THE MISSISSIPPI
Source: Lake Itasca, Minnesota
Sea: Gulf of Mexico
Journey: 3,705 km (2,302 miles)

THE THAMES
Source: Cotswolds, England
Sea: North Sea
Journey: 340 km (210 miles)

THE YANGTZE
Source: Kunlun Mountains, western China
Sea: Pacific Ocean
Journey: 6,300 km (3,915 miles)

THE DANUBE
Source: Black Forest, Germany
Sea: Black Sea
Journey: 2,850 km (1,771 miles)

WHICH MIDDLE CIRCLE IS BIGGEST?

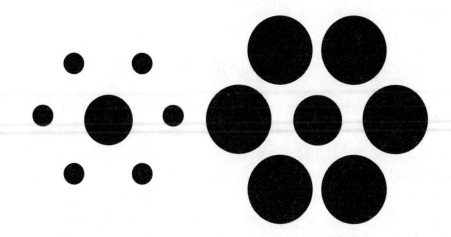

Answer: They are both the same size.

HOW TO HYPNOTIZE A CHICKEN

Note: No aniamls are harmed during this experiement, not even their diginity is shaken - unless you get the chicken to run around like human and that's just mean.

There are seveal ways to lure a chicken into a trance, and this is just one of them. The most important thing you must remember is to be gentle and quiet to achieve hypnosis.

1. Place a chicken on a flat surface, laying on its side with one wing underneath its body. Gently hold the chicken still, with its head flat against the surface.

2. Keep holding the chicken still with one hand and use a finger from the other hand to trace a line, about 30 cm (1 ft) long, from the beak-tip and along the surface in front of its eyes. Repeat this until the chicken is in a trance.

3. The trance may last seconds or hours but any sudden noise or movement will bring the chicken out of its trance and send it flapping and squawking away.

LIFE ON MARS

The surface of Mars is thought to be mainly composed of a black volcanic rock called basalt, which is also found on Earth.

In December 1984, a Martian meteorite was found in Antarctica. It is thought to have contained fossils of microscopic bacteria that lived on Mars millions of years ago.

In 2004, the orbiting probe Mars Express found methane in the Martian atmosphere. On Earth, methane is emitted by primitive life forms.

TV FIRSTS

1926   Scottish engineer John Logie Baird gives the first public demonstration of a working television set in London.

1951   The world's first colour programme is broadcast in the USA. It is a musical variety show.

1955   The first wireless remote control is launched. It is called the 'Zenith Flash-matic'.

1964   The plasma display monitor is invented.

1967   The first video game for a TV is launched, called *Chase*.

1969   A camera in the lunar module provides live TV coverage of Neil Armstrong becoming the first man to walk on the Moon. Approximately 600 million people tune in.

1975   Sony launch the 'Betamax' home recording system. The system allows consumers to record and play back television programmes.

1975   The band Queen produce the first successful pop video. It is to their song *Bohemian Rhapsody*.

1976   The Japanese company JVC launch the 'VHS' home recording system to rival Sony's 'Betamax'.

1996   The first DVD players and discs are sold in Japan.

1998   The first High Definition TVs go on sale in America.

2006   The first fully developed Blu-Ray DVD player goes on sale.

2010   The first 3-D TVs are available to buy.

SPY CODE

Ears Only................Documents too secret to commit to writing

Eyes Only................Documents that may be read but not discussed

Wet Job................An operation in which blood is shed

Dead Drop................Secret locations where messages are left

Black Operations................Secret operations that no one owns up to

Mole................An agent sent to gather intelligence by working or living among the enemy

PATRON SAINT OF ...

Maria Goretti...Girls

John Bosco..Boys

Roch..Dogs

Francis of Assisi...Animals

Gabriel of Our Lady of Sorrows..............................Students

Amand...Scouts

Joseph of Cupertino..Astronauts

Fiacre..Taxi drivers

Isidore of Seville............................Computer programmers

Clare of Assisi...Television

Barbara..Fireworks

Francis de Sales...Teachers

THE PERPETUALLY ASCENDING STAIRCASE

Answer to stick puzzle on page 209

ARE YOU TELEPATHIC?

1. Get a friend to sit in front of you with a pack of playing cards.
2. Ask them to pick one card at random, without letting you see it. Then tell them to concentrate really hard on that card.
3. Close your eyes and empty your mind, allowing your brain to 'receive' your friend's telepathic message.
4. Shout out the number and suit of the first card that comes to your mind and see if you are correct.

> In May 2005, a US hot-dog company made a 22.9-m- (75-ft-) long hot dog, some 120 times longer than your average sausage.

MEDIEVAL WEAPONS

Knight's sword..Single-handed, cross-shaped sword

Claymore...........................Large, two-handed sword used in clan warfare

Sabre...Curved sword with large hand guard

Bludgeon.............................One- or two-handed club for whacking things

War hammer............Hammer with one blunt end and one spiked end

Pike.....................Long, spear-like weapon used against cavalry assaults

Arbalest..Large, tremendously powerful crossbow

Flail...........................Spiked metal ball(s) attached to a handle by a chain

Morning star........Pole with a spherical head with a large spike on its end, and smaller spikes around its circumference

THE GEORGE WASHINGTON CONUNDRUM

When he was a boy, the person who became the first President of the USA allegedly cut down his father's cherry tree. The axe he used is on display in a museum, although, having had both its handle and head replaced several times, no part of the original axe remains.

SOME SUCCESSFUL MARS PROBES

Mars 3...USSR, launched 1971

Mariner 9..USA, launched 1971

Viking 1...USA, launched 1975

Mars Pathfinder...USA, launched 1996

Mars Odyssey...USA, launched 2001

Beagle 2..Europe, launched 2003

Opportunity..USA, launched 2003

Phoenix Mars Lander..USA, launched 2007

Curiosity..USA, launched 2011

MOM...India, launched 2013

PRO-WRESTLING MOVES

Armbreaker • Atomic Drop

Powerslam • Twist of Fate

Brainbuster • Body Slam

Death Valley Driver

Russian Legsweep

Frankensteiner

Huracarrana

Irish Whip

Facebreaker

Electric Chair Bomb

NOT ALLOWED IN AMERICA

Milking another person's cow (Texas).

Getting a fish drunk (Ohio).

Donkeys sleeping in bathtubs (Arizona).

Unmarried women parachuting on Sundays (Florida).

Taking a bite from another person's hamburger (Oklahoma).

Singing in a public place when wearing a swimsuit (Florida).

Carrying an ice-cream cone in your back pocket (Alabama).

Wearing a false moustache that may cause people to laugh in church (Alabama).

ANIMAL SIXTH SENSE

AMPULLAE OF LORENZI
This special organ enables sharks to detect weak electrical stimuli from the muscle movements of prey that are hidden or distant.

BUTTERFLY TARSI
The 'tarsi', or feet, of the American painted lady have special sensors that allow the butterfly to detect sweet food.

LATERAL LINE
Fish use this sense organ to detect changes in water pressure and feel the movement of other animals in the water nearby.

JACOBSEN'S ORGAN
Snakes use this organ to 'taste' prey. Their forked tongues collect chemicals from the air and bring them into the mouth, where the organ is located.

A hair transplant involves the removal of a patch of hairy scalp from the head. Hundreds of individual hairs or hair clusters are then taken from the patch under a magnifying glass and sewn back into the scalp to cover the bald area.

AN ETHICAL PROBLEM

A runaway train is hurtling towards five people tied to a railway track. You can save them by pulling a lever that steers the train down a branch line. Unfortunately, there is a single person tied to the branch line. Do you pull the lever?

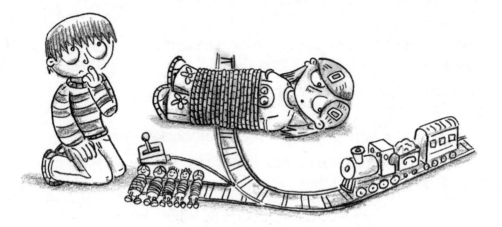

INTERNATIONAL DIALLING CODES

Antarctica...+672

Australia...+61

France..+33

Germany..+49

Greece...+30

Italy..+39

Mongolia..+976

Netherlands...+31

Poland...+48

Spain...+34

Switzerland...+41

UK..+44

USA..+1

HOW TO INSULT SOMEONE AND GET AWAY WITH IT

Memorize these handy put-downs which you can use in all sorts of situations. Your family, friends and teachers will be so amazed by your impressive vocabulary, that you won't even get into trouble.

Abhorrent (ab-hor-uhnt) - disgusting:
'The state of my brother's bedroom is abhorrent.'

Asinine (ass-in-ine) - very stupid:
'That was an asinine thing to do.'

Decrepit (di-krep-it) - very old and feeble:
'Teacher is so decrepit, I'm amazed he's still alive.'

Disingenuous (dis-in-jen-yoo-uhs) - insincere, false:
'Your excuses are rather disingenuous.'

Fatuous (fach-oo-uhs) - foolish:
'I am tired of your fatuous jokes.'

Malevolent (muh-lev-uh-luhnt) - mean, spiteful:
'You are the most malevolent person in this school.'

Malodorous (mal-oh-der-uhs) - smelly, stinky:
*'Your dog is the most malodorous
I have ever had the misfortune to encounter.'*

Ninnyhammer (nin-ee-ham-er) - a fool:
'What a ninnyhammer my sister is!'

Peurile (pyoo-er-il) - childish, immature:
'That was such a puerile thing to say.'

The goliath bird-eating spider, a type of tarantula living in the South American jungle, is recorded as the world's biggest spider. It has a leg span of around 28 cm (11 in).

20TH-CENTURY TOYS

1900.................................Plasticine

1902.................................Teddy bear

1913................Crossword puzzle

1921................................Pogo stick

1943...............................Silly putty

1946..........................Slinky spring

1948...................................Frisbee

1958............................Skateboard

1958.......................................Lego

1975..........................Rubik's Cube

1996.............................Tamagotchi

1998.....................................Furby

TONGUE TWISTERS

'Peter Piper picked a peck of pickled peppers.
A peck of pickled peppers Peter Piper picked.
If Peter Piper picked a peck of pickled peppers,
where's the peck of pickled peppers Peter Piper picked?'

'How much wood would a woodchuck chuck
if a woodchuck could chuck wood?
He would chuck, he would, as much as he could,
and chuck as much wood as a woodchuck would
if a woodchuck could chuck wood.'

'Red lorry, yellow lorry, red lorry, yellow lorry.'

'Sam's shop stocks short spotted socks.'

'A noisy noise annoys an oyster.'

'Just think, that sphinx has a sphincter that stinks!'

'Six slippery snails slid slowly seaward.'

'Which witch wished which wicked wish?'

'Many an anemone sees an enemy anemone.'

PALMISTRY

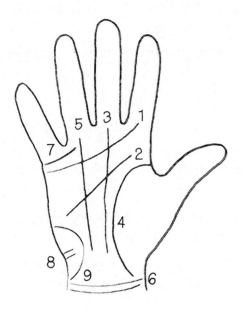

1. HEART LINE
Straight: Romantic
Long: Outgoing
Short: Shy

2. HEAD LINE
Curved: Spontaneous
Straight: Practical
Deep: Imaginative

3. FATE LINE
To have a fate line
shows a sense of
responsibility
and purpose.

4. LIFE LINE
Long: Vitality for life
Short: Good health
Weak: Indecisive

5. SUN LINE
Short: Success in the future
Long: Wealth and happiness
Ends in a star shape: Fame

6. LUCK LINE
Clear line: 30 years of luck
Gaps in line: Less fortunate
periods in life

7. RELATIONSHIP LINE
Long, horizontal line:
One dominant,
happy relationship
More than one line: Several
relationships affect your life
Curves upward at
the end: A successful
relationship
Curves downward at the
end: A difficult ending

8. TRAVEL LINES
The more you have, the
greater your desire to travel.

9. INTUITIVE LINE
Having this line means
you are impulsive.

THE COLOURS OF A RAINBOW

Red • Orange • Yellow
Green • Blue • Indigo • Violet

MAGIC HANDCUFF TRICK

You will need: a piece of rope about 1-m (3-ft) long, a large scarf, two identical bangles, a long-sleeved top.

Set-up: slide one bangle up your arm, making certain it is hidden beneath your sleeve.

PERFORMANCE

1. Ask two helpers to tie the ends of the rope to your wrists.

2. Ask one helper to pass you the bangle, then tell the audience that you will make this appear on the rope with your hands still tied.

3. Tell your helpers to cover your hands with the scarf. They should continue to hold up the ends of the scarf.

4. With your hands out of sight, hide the bangle in your pocket or under your clothes. Then slide the hidden bangle down your sleeve on top of the rope.

5. Now ask your helpers to take the scarf away. Hold up your arms and show the bangle dangling from the rope.

Egyptians often brought a giant mummy to banquets to remind everyone that death was never far away.

THE TEN DEADLIEST SNAKES

FIERCE SNAKE (Australia)
The toxic venom from
one bite would be enough
to kill 100 people.

BROWN SNAKE (Australia)
A drop of venom, smaller
than a grain of salt, could
kill a person.

MALAYAN KRAIT (Asia
and Indonesia)
Fifty per cent of bite
victims have died, even
after treatment.

TIGER SNAKE (Australia)
Extremely aggressive, kills
more people than any
other snake in Australia.

SAW-SCALED VIPER (Africa)
Kills more people than all
other venomous African
snakes combined.

BOOMSLANG (Africa)
Has very long fangs
and can open its mouth
a full 180° to bite.

CORAL SNAKE (USA)
Extremely potent venom
but fangs are typically
too small to pierce
human skin.

DEATH ADDER (Australia
and New Guinea)
Can deliver enough venom
in one bite to kill 18 people.

BEAKED SEA SNAKE (Asia)
Responsible for more
than half of all cases
of sea snake bites, ninety
per cent of which are fatal.

TAIPAN (Australia)
The venom from one bite
can kill 12,000 guinea pigs.

HOW TO PROTECT YOURSELF FROM A VAMPIRE IN THE MODERN WORLD

RINGING BELLS - Bells are known to drive away the undead. Try using a trilling ringtone on your mobile phone.

BLACK DOGS - Some believe black dogs are the enemies of vampires, others believe they may act as vampire assistants. Avoid them completely by getting your parents to buy you a ginger tabby or a gerbil instead.

KNOTS - Knotted string around doorways or on graves distracts vampires, because they allegedly feel compelled to untangle it. Hang your trainers from the bedroom door. The smell will also put them off and they are more likely to try elsewhere, like your parents' room.

GARLIC - The classic vampire deterrent is a bulb of garlic worn around the neck or rubbed around doors or windows. Eating garlic bread or chicken kievs may be just as effective.

HOLLY or JUNIPER - Keeping branches of certain trees in the house will deter vampires. Leave a branch on the floor for them to trip over in the dark.

SUNLIGHT - Vampires dissolve into dust as soon as a sunbeam hits them. If you can't wait till sunrise, try hitting them with your bedside lamp.

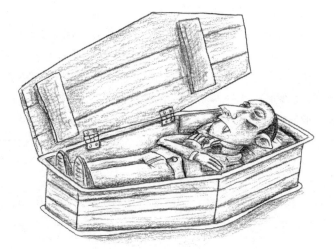

EGG-STRAORDINARY

Of all birds, the kiwi lays the largest egg in proportion to its body size, sometimes weighing more than a quarter of its body weight.

An ostrich egg is 24 times larger than a hen's egg. It takes 42 minutes to boil, 80 minutes to hard boil and a man can stand on the shell without it cracking.

Add sugar to a glass of water, then put an egg into the water. The egg will float.

The incubation temperature of turtle and tortoise eggs directly influences the sex of the hatchling.

The female egg cell is the largest of all cells in the human body.

WHO'S AFRAID OF THE DENTIST?

The first dentists in Japan perfected special finger exercises so they could pull teeth with their bare hands.

Tooth drawers in ancient China used to spend hours pulling out nails hammered into planks of wood, as practice for extracting teeth with their fingers.

The first dentist's drill was driven by a wheel. It tended to vary in speed and sometimes stopped mid-operation.

It wasn't until 1872 that the first, efficient rotary dental drill was introduced.

INDEX

ANIMALS

ART

BIRDS

INDEX

INDEX

INDEX

INDEX

HUMAN BODY

INDEX

INSECTS

INVENTIONS

INDEX

INDEX

INDEX

MUSIC

MYTHOLOGY

INDEX

INDEX

INDEX

INDEX

GOODBYE

So long

Farewell

Cheerio

Ta ta

See you later, alligator

In a while, crocodile

Also available:

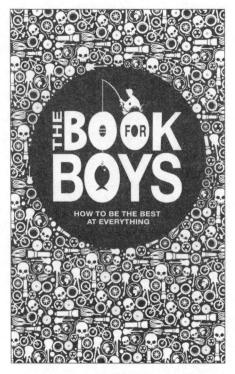

ISBN: 978-1-78055-194-4

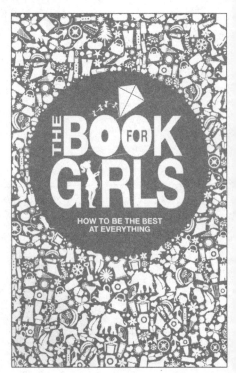

ISBN: 978-1-78055-195-1